THE ULTIMATE BREAKUP WORKBOOK:

HOW TO GET OVER YOUR EX

TRANSFORMATIVE EXERCISES, CBT SKILLS, AND EMPOWERING SELF-LOVE PRACTICES TO RECLAIM JOY, FIND INNER PEACE, AND EMBRACE YOUR NEW BEGINNING

DYLAN WALKER

YOUR FREE GIFT

As a way of saying thanks for your purchase, I'm offering the book Overcoming Limiting Beliefs for FREE to my readers.
To get instant access just go to:

https://dylanwalkerbooks.com/selflove-free-bonus

Inside the book, you will discover:

- ➤ **10 steps to break through your limiting beliefs**: Even if you struggled with negative thinking before, this book will be the change you need.

- ➤ **An action plan to end sabotaging yourself**: Learn exactly how to reframe your thoughts with just 10-minutes a day.

- ➤ **Reduce stress and achieve unshakable confidence**: A healthy mindset leads to achieving your goals and dreams. It's time to take back your life!

If you want to stop negative thinking and start making progress towards your dreams make sure to grab the free book.

TABLE OF CONTENTS

PART 3: A BETTER YOU

INTRODUCTION

Have you ever experienced that gut-wrenching feeling after a breakup? That sensation of your heart sinking into the depths of despair? Or the relentless tears that seem to have no end? If you've ever been through the pain of heartbreak, you know exactly what I'm talking about. It's a pain that can shatter your world, leaving you feeling lost, alone, and emotionally vulnerable. It's a pain that many of us have encountered at some point in our lives, and yet, it remains one of the most challenging emotions to navigate.

If you find yourself struggling to overcome heartbreak, are feeling trapped in a cycle of sadness and longing, and desperately searching for a way to heal, then you've come to the right place. This book is designed to be your guiding light in the darkest of times. It offers a modern and simplistic approach to help you unlock your highest potential, achieve your deepest desires, and embark on a journey of self-healing and growth.

I understand that you're going through a tough time right now. Maybe you've recently gone through a breakup, and the pain feels unbearable. The sadness, grief, loneliness, or rejection you are experiencing might be overwhelming. Perhaps you're struggling with low self-worth or self-esteem, finding it difficult to move on from the broken relationship. It's possible that you have a history of toxic or unhealthy relationships and they have left you feeling lost and emotionally scarred.

The pain of heartbreak can be all-consuming, affecting various aspects of your life, such as your work, friendships, and overall well-being. It can be like a dark cloud that hovers over you, making it hard to see a way out. But fear not, for there is a solution! This book will be your detailed guide to creating and maintaining your emotional well-being. It is not a mere textbook filled with complex jargon; rather, it's an easily digestible, step-by-step journey to help you navigate the stormy waters of heartbreak.

You might be wondering why you should trust this book to guide you through such a personal and challenging journey. As the author of this book, I come to you with a genuine passion for helping people overcome relationship issues, especially those pertaining to heartbreak. Over the last five years, I have immersed myself in studying the best methods for healing after heartbreak and avoiding emotional trauma. My goal is to provide you with a toolkit that is easy to grasp, not overly textbook-like, and yet not too basic for your needs.

But it's not just about academic knowledge. I've had my fair share of struggles with heartbreak and I've made mistakes along the way. There was a time when I felt completely lost, unable to cope with the pain and uncertainty. Yet, those very mistakes have shaped my expertise in this field, and now I am sharing what I know so that you don't have to go through the same painful journey.

I vividly recall the nights of endless tears, the moments of self-doubt, and the overwhelming sense of loss. However, as I navigated my way through the labyrinth of heartbreak, I discovered powerful techniques that helped me heal and grow. Through journaling, self-love exercises, and the practice of Cognitive Behavioral Therapy (CBT), I found a path to reclaim my sense of self, cultivate healthier relationships, and embrace a brighter future.

By embarking on this journey with me, you will gain an advantage as a beginner in the world of practical self-love techniques. This book is not just a collection of theories; rather, it's a toolkit filled with real, actionable exercises and prompts to help you heal, grow, and find inner peace.

Don't let heartbreak hold you back any longer. Start your learning right away, and the next time you come face-to-face with a breakup, you'll know exactly what to do. It's essential to understand how to overcome heartbreak and pain, especially at this time, to avoid feeling lost and overwhelmed.

So, are you ready to discover how to overcome heartbreak and pain and start your journey to healing and growth? Keep reading, and I hope you enjoy the insights and exercises that await you in these pages.

Heartbreak is a painful but transformative experience. As you progress through the chapters of this book, you will find a collection of practical tools, self-love exercises, CBT techniques, and emotional healing practices that will empower you to overcome heartbreak and pain and find inner peace. Let this workbook be your trusted companion on the path to healing. It will guide you every step of the way.

Remember, healing takes time and effort, but with the right tools and mindset, you will emerge stronger and more resilient than ever before. So, take a deep breath, trust the process, and embrace the transformative power of healing after heartbreak.

Are you ready to embark on your journey of healing and growth? Let's begin this transformative adventure together.

PART 1:

UNDERSTANDING THE PAIN

Heartbreak is an emotion that knows no boundaries, affecting individuals from all walks of life. It can strike unexpectedly, leaving us feeling shattered and vulnerable. In Part 1, we will explore the reasons why heartbreak hurts so intensely and why it's essential to acknowledge and embrace our feelings during this tumultuous time.

We will take a closer look at the role of self-love in the healing process. Understanding that healing starts from within, and that self-compassion is an integral part of our journey will set the stage for profound personal growth.

CHAPTER 1:
FACING HEARTBREAK

As we navigate through the tumultuous waves of heartbreak, we will uncover the raw emotions that lie beneath the surface. We will delve into the psychological and physiological aspects of heartbreak, seeking to grasp the roots of this profound pain.

In this chapter, we will also delve into why finding healing after heartbreak is of utmost importance. It is a journey of self-discovery and self-compassion, an opportunity to nurture the very essence of who we are. Despite the pain, it is crucial to embrace this opportunity, for in healing lies the key to unlocking our highest potential.

So, let us embark on this chapter together, fearlessly facing heartbreak, and embracing the profound lessons it has to offer.

Addicted to Love

Love has long been regarded as a powerful and transformative emotion, capable of bringing immense joy and happiness into our lives. It ignites a fire within us, fills our hearts with warmth, and makes us feel alive. However, beneath its enchanting allure, there exists a phenomenon that researchers and experts have come to recognize as "love addiction." This concept suggests that being in love can trigger addictive tendencies, leading individuals to become emotionally dependent on their partners and the feelings of euphoria associated with love.

Numerous studies and articles have delved into the fascinating topic of love addiction, shedding light on its similarities to substance addiction and its impact on our mental well-being. As we explore this concept, it becomes evident that love, much like drugs, can create a potent chemical cocktail within our brains that fosters feelings of pleasure and reward. The heightened levels of dopamine and oxytocin, often referred to as the "love hormones," can create a state of euphoria and attachment to our romantic partners.

One notable study, as reported by *Discover* magazine, found that when individuals who were deeply in love were shown pictures of their beloved, brain regions associated with addiction and reward were activated (Fisher, 2023). This fascinating link between love and addiction offers a glimpse into the powerful hold that love can have on our minds and hearts.

But how do we distinguish between genuine, healthy love and love addiction? According to experts, love addiction is characterized by an obsessive and compulsive need for love and validation, often leading to emotional turmoil and codependent behaviors (Fisher, 2023). Individuals experiencing love addiction may find it challenging to establish a sense of self outside of their relationships, and their happiness becomes heavily reliant on the presence and validation of their partners.

As discussed in Mental Help, one of the indicators of love addiction is an intense fear of abandonment, driving individuals to cling to their partners and relationships even when they are detrimental to their well-being (Livingstone, 2011). The fear of being alone can lead to staying in toxic relationships, perpetuating a cycle of emotional pain and dependence.

Recognizing the signs of love addiction is crucial, as it can hinder personal growth and lead to unhealthy relationship patterns. By understanding the similarities between love and addiction, individuals can begin to address their emotional dependency and embark on a journey of self-discovery and healing.

Healing from Love Addiction

In the context of heartbreak, love addiction can magnify the pain and difficulty of moving on from a broken relationship. When love becomes an addiction, the withdrawal from a romantic partner can be agonizing, leading to feelings of emptiness and despair. The fear of losing the source of validation and happiness can become overwhelming, making it challenging to let go and find closure.

However, recognizing and addressing love addiction is the first step towards healing and regaining control of one's emotional well-being. It is essential to understand that love addiction is not a sign of weakness or inadequacy; rather, it is a human response to the intense emotions that love can evoke.

By cultivating self-love and building a strong foundation of self-worth, you will become better equipped to navigate the complexities of heartbreak and heal from the pain it brings.

Cultivating Self-Love and Emotional Resilience

One of the most powerful tools in overcoming love addiction is self-love. Learning to value and appreciate yourself outside of romantic relationships can provide a sense of fulfillment and emotional resilience. Through various self-love exercises and practices, you can discover the importance of nurturing your emotional well-being and prioritizing your needs.

Incorporating mindfulness techniques and self-compassion into your healing journey can also be beneficial. Practicing mindfulness allows you to be present in the moment, acknowledge your feelings without judgment, and build emotional awareness. This heightened emotional intelligence can help you navigate the ups and downs of heartbreak with grace and self-awareness.

Breaking Free from Codependent Patterns

Codependency is often intertwined with love addiction, where individuals become enmeshed with their partners, sacrificing their needs for the sake of the relationship.

Recognizing the importance of independence and self-reliance can empower you to create healthier and more balanced connections with others. By setting boundaries and communicating your needs effectively, you will foster a sense of agency and control over your emotional well-being.

Navigating the Path to Healing

Healing from love addiction and heartbreak is not a linear process; it is a journey of self-discovery, growth, and self-compassion. As you progress through *The Ultimate Breakup Workbook*, you will gain valuable insights into your emotional landscape, allowing you to confront your pain and embrace the transformative power of healing.

Remember, healing takes time and effort, but with the right tools and mindset, you will emerge stronger and more resilient than ever before. By addressing love addiction and cultivating self-love, you will pave the way to a healthier and more fulfilling future.

Embrace the opportunity to heal and grow, for in understanding and overcoming love addiction lies the key to unlocking your highest potential. Let us embark on this transformative journey together, breaking free from the chains of emotional dependency and embracing a path of self-love, healing, and personal growth.

Like Every Other Addiction, Withdrawal Breaks You

When we think of addiction and withdrawal, we often associate them with substances like drugs or alcohol. However, the emotional rollercoaster of heartbreak can be just as powerful, leading to withdrawal symptoms that bear striking similarities to substance withdrawal. The pain and turmoil of a breakup can create a void, leaving us feeling lost, broken, and emotionally depleted.

Understanding the Withdrawal

When we experience love and attachment, our brains release neurotransmitters like dopamine and oxytocin, which foster feelings of pleasure and bonding. The euphoria of being in love is akin to the highs experienced with addictive substances. However, when that love is taken away—through a breakup or separation—our brain chemistry undergoes a dramatic shift.

As reported by *Sandstone Care*, withdrawal from love can lead to symptoms such as insomnia, loss of appetite, increased anxiety, and intense cravings for the person we once loved (Quinn, 2022). The brain's reward system, which was flooded with feel-good chemicals during the relationship, is now deprived of those rewards, resulting in a sense of emotional withdrawal.

In a way, our brains become dependent on the emotional high of being with our partner, and the sudden absence of that high can be distressing.

We may find ourselves constantly reminiscing about the past, longing for the feelings of happiness and connection we once experienced. The pain of withdrawal can be all-consuming, leaving us feeling vulnerable and emotionally raw.

The Breakup as a Drug Withdrawal

A breakup's impact on our brains is so profound that it can evoke physical responses similar to drug withdrawal. In an article by *SBS Insight*, Dr. Helen Fisher, an anthropologist and expert on love, explains that romantic love activates the brain's reward system in the same way drugs do (Wilson, 2018). Therefore, when that love is lost, our brain's chemistry changes, resulting in feelings of craving and withdrawal.

In *The Cut*, Dr. Lucy Brown, a neuroscientist, emphasizes that the brain regions activated during a breakup are the same as those associated with physical pain (Baer, 2017). This finding reinforces the idea that heartbreak is not just an emotional experience but also one that can trigger physical responses.

Navigating the Path to Healing

Understanding that heartbreak can create withdrawal-like symptoms can be validating, as it helps us recognize that what we're feeling is a natural response to loss. Healing after a breakup involves allowing ourselves to grieve and acknowledge our emotions without judgment.

Through self-compassion, mindfulness, and emotional self-care, you will begin to find solace amidst the storm of emotions.

Through self-rediscovery, self-love, and personal growth, you will emerge stronger, more resilient, and ready to embrace a brighter future. Remember, you are not alone on this journey, and with every step, you are one step closer to healing and emotional freedom.

The Science of Heartbreak

Love, with all its enchanting allure, has the power to lift us to new heights of joy and happiness. However, when that love is lost, it can also plunge us into the depths of emotional pain and heartbreak. As we navigate the turbulent waters of heartbreak, it is essential to understand the scientific underpinnings of why heartbreak hurts so much.

The Brain's Response to Heartbreak

When we fall in love, our brains release a flood of neurotransmitters and hormones that create feelings of euphoria, pleasure, and bonding. Dopamine, oxytocin, and serotonin are some of the key chemicals involved in this emotional cocktail, fueling the joy and connection we feel with our romantic partners.

However, when a relationship comes to an end, the brain's chemistry undergoes a dramatic shift. As reported by *Live Science*, negative emotions such as rejection and heartbreak activate brain regions associated with physical pain (Mudge, 2023). These regions, including the anterior cingulate cortex and insula, process both emotional and physical pain, blurring the lines between the two. The brain struggles to differentiate between emotional pain and physical pain, leading people to feel a deep sense of hurt and loss.

The Impact on Our Bodies

The science of heartbreak also extends to its impact on our bodies. Heartbreak triggers the body's stress response, leading to an increase in the stress hormone cortisol. Elevated cortisol levels can lead to a variety of physical symptoms, including sleep disturbances, appetite changes, and weakened immune function.

The physical toll of heartbreak is not to be underestimated, as the physical sensations can exacerbate feelings of sadness and loneliness. The combination of emotional pain and physical symptoms can create a cycle of distress, making it challenging to move forward after a breakup.

Coping with Heartbreak through Science

While heartbreak is a natural and inevitable part of the human experience, understanding its scientific basis can provide us with insights to cope and heal.

Mindfulness practices, for instance, can help regulate emotional responses and promote emotional resilience during heartbreak. By focusing on the present moment without judgment, you can begin to detach from the pain of the past and embrace a sense of self-compassion.

The Different Types of Heartbreak

Heartbreak is a complex and multifaceted emotional experience that can take various forms, each leaving a unique mark on our hearts and souls. As we journey through life and love, we encounter different types of heartbreak that test our resilience and shape our understanding of relationships.

In our 20s, a time of exploration and self-discovery, heartbreak can manifest in diverse ways. These various forms of heartbreak offer us valuable lessons and opportunities for growth. Let us explore some of the different types of heartbreak that we may undoubtedly experience in our 20s (and beyond):

1. First Love Heartbreak

First love heartbreak is a rite of passage that many individuals experience in their 20s. It is a poignant and intense form of heartbreak that shapes our perceptions of love and relationships. The end of our first love can feel like the end of the world as we navigate the unfamiliar territory of loss and emotional pain.

2. Long-Term Relationship Breakup

The breakup of a long-term relationship in our 20s can be particularly challenging, as it often involves the dismantling of a significant chapter of our lives. The emotions tied to shared memories and future plans can leave us feeling adrift and uncertain about our path forward.

3. Unrequited Love Heartbreak

Unrequited love is a heartbreak born from one-sided affection, where our feelings are not reciprocated by the person we love. The pain of unrequited love can be all-consuming, leaving us questioning our worth and longing for a love that may never be.

4. On-and-Off Relationship Heartbreak

This type of heartbreak is characterized by the cyclical nature of breaking up and reconciling. The emotional rollercoaster of this type of heartbreak can be exhausting as we grapple with conflicting emotions and uncertainty about the future.

5. Friendship-Turned-Romance Heartbreak

When a close friendship evolves into a romantic relationship and subsequently ends, it can result in a unique form of heartbreak. The loss of both a romantic partner and a close friend can leave us feeling doubly bereft.

6. Distance-Induced Heartbreak

Distance-induced heartbreak occurs when geographical or logistical challenges separate two people in a relationship. The strain of maintaining a long-distance relationship can lead to heartache and the difficult decision of whether to continue or let go.

7. Infatuation Heartbreak

Infatuation heartbreak arises from intense feelings for someone that do not develop into a deeper emotional connection. The realization that our infatuation may not lead to a lasting relationship can be disheartening.

8. Mutual Breakup

The mutual breakup involves both partners acknowledging that their relationship is no longer fulfilling and deciding to part ways amicably. While less tumultuous than other types of heartbreak, it still carries its share of sadness and adjustment.

9. Betrayal Heartbreak

Betrayal heartbreak stems from discovering a breach of trust within a relationship, such as infidelity or deceit. Coping with the emotional fallout of betrayal can be deeply painful and requires rebuilding trust in future relationships.

10. Self-Discovery Heartbreak

Sometimes, heartbreak emerges from the need to prioritize personal growth and self-discovery. Choosing to focus on oneself and end a relationship can lead to heartache but also pave the way for transformative growth.

The Stages of Breakup

A breakup is an emotional journey that takes us through a series of stages, each characterized by a unique set of feelings and challenges. As we navigate the aftermath of a breakup, it is essential to understand and embrace these stages, allowing ourselves to process our emotions and embark on the path to healing.

1. Denial and Shock

The initial stage of a breakup is often marked by denial and shock. It can be challenging to accept that the relationship has come to an end, leaving us feeling numb and disoriented. Our minds may struggle to comprehend the reality of the situation, leading to a sense of disbelief.

2. Anger and Resentment

As reality sets in, we may begin to experience feelings of anger and resentment. We might direct these emotions towards our ex-partner, ourselves, or the circumstances that led to the breakup. Anger can be a natural response to loss, signaling our emotional investment in the relationship.

3. Bargaining and Guilt

In this stage, we might find ourselves bargaining with the universe or seeking ways to reverse the breakup. We may experience guilt over past actions or wonder if there was anything we could have done differently to save the relationship. It is crucial to recognize that some things are beyond our control, and self-compassion is essential during this time.

4. Sadness and Depression

The sadness and depression stages are a significant part of the healing process. It is normal to grieve the loss of a meaningful relationship, and these emotions may come in waves. During this stage, it is essential to reach out to support systems and engage in self-care activities that promote emotional well-being.

5. Acceptance and Understanding

As we move through the stages of grief, we begin to reach a place of acceptance and understanding. Acceptance does not necessarily mean that we are over the relationship entirely; rather, it signifies a willingness to acknowledge the reality of the situation and take steps towards healing.

6. Self-Rediscovery and Growth

The self-rediscovery and growth stage is a transformative phase of the breakup journey. During this time, we may explore new hobbies, interests, and aspects of ourselves that were perhaps overshadowed during the relationship. It is a time of personal growth and empowerment.

7. Renewed Hope and Moving Forward

As we progress through the stages of a breakup, we start to find renewed hope for the future. We become more open to the idea of new possibilities and relationships, recognizing that heartbreak does not define our worth or potential for love.

Navigating the Stages of a Breakup

As you journey through the stages of a breakup, remember that you are not alone. Heartbreak is a shared human experience, and by embracing these stages, you will find the strength and resilience to heal and embrace a brighter future.

Identifying Unresolved Feelings and Emotions

Unresolved feelings and emotions from the past can linger within us, influencing our present experiences and relationships. These unresolved issues may stem from past traumas, past relationships, or unprocessed emotions that were never fully addressed.

The Impact of Unresolved Feelings

Unresolved feelings can manifest in various ways, impacting our emotional well-being and behavior. They may cause us to repeat harmful patterns in relationships, struggle with trust and intimacy, or harbor feelings of anger, sadness, or resentment. Recognizing the presence of unresolved emotions is crucial, as they can hinder our ability to heal and move forward after a breakup.

Tracing the Roots

To identify unresolved feelings, we may need to trace their roots back to past experiences or relationships. Unresolved issues can originate from childhood experiences, previous heartbreaks, or significant life events that left emotional imprints on our psyche. By understanding the origins of these feelings, we can begin to untangle the emotional knots that have been holding us back.

Recognizing Patterns in Relationships

Unresolved feelings often manifest in patterns that emerge within our relationships. These patterns may include avoiding emotional intimacy, seeking validation from partners, or experiencing difficulty trusting others. By recognizing these patterns, we can gain insight into the underlying unresolved emotions driving our behaviors.

The Connection Between Unresolved Feelings and Addiction

Unresolved feelings can also be closely linked to addiction. Substance abuse and addictive behaviors are sometimes used as coping mechanisms to numb the pain of unresolved emotions. Addressing these underlying feelings is essential for long-term recovery and healing.

The Importance of Processing Emotions

Avoiding or suppressing emotions can prolong the healing process and lead to more significant emotional turmoil in the future. By acknowledging and processing our feelings, we can begin to release the emotional weight that has been holding us back.

Seeking Support and Professional Help

Identifying and addressing unresolved feelings can be a challenging and emotional process. It is essential to seek support from friends, family, or professionals. A therapist or counselor can provide guidance and tools to navigate these emotions and facilitate healing.

The Healing Process: Long, Yet Important

Healing after a breakup is a journey that unfolds at its own pace. It is a process that requires time, patience, and self-compassion.

The Timeline of Healing

There is no one-size-fits-all timeline for healing after a breakup. The duration of the healing process can vary widely from person to person. Factors such as the length of the relationship, the depth of emotional attachment, and individual coping mechanisms can influence how long it takes to move forward.

Understanding Grief

Grief is an integral part of the healing process. When a relationship ends, we grieve not only the loss of the partnership but also the dreams and future we envisioned with our ex-partner. This grief may come in waves, and it is essential to allow ourselves to feel and process these emotions fully.

Seeking Professional Support

As we navigate the healing process, seeking support from a therapist or counselor can be immensely beneficial. Many therapists emphasize the importance of seeking professional help to work through complex emotions and gain insights into ourselves. A therapist can provide valuable tools and coping strategies to facilitate healing.

Letting Go of Comparisons

It is crucial to avoid comparing our healing process to that of others. Each individual's journey is unique and focusing on someone else's progress may lead to unnecessary pressure or self-criticism. Embrace your own path and trust that healing will come in due time.

Embracing Self-Discovery

During the healing process, we have the opportunity to rediscover ourselves and our passions. As we heal from heartbreak, we may find that we grow stronger, more self-aware, and more resilient.

The Importance of Healing

Healing after a breakup is not only about moving on from the past but also about preparing ourselves for healthier and more fulfilling relationships in the future. The significance of healing is often emphasized, as it enables us to break free from the emotional burdens of the past and approach new relationships with a clearer perspective.

CHAPTER 2:
SELF-LOVE FOR THE HEALING JOURNEY

In the aftermath of heartbreak, when emotions are raw and vulnerabilities are exposed, there lies a profound truth: the journey to healing begins with self-love. This chapter is a guide to the essential concept of self-love and its pivotal role in the process of healing after heartbreak. As we delve into the intricacies of this chapter, we'll explore how embracing self-love can be the cornerstone of your healing journey, igniting the transformative power that allows you to reclaim your sense of self and move forward with renewed strength and purpose.

Tips for Getting Over a Breakup

Navigating the terrain of a breakup can feel like traversing uncharted waters, but rest assured, you are not alone in your journey. This chapter offers a collection of invaluable tips gathered from experts and those who have walked this path before, aiming to guide you towards healing and renewal. As you immerse yourself in these tips, remember that healing is a personal process, and these suggestions can be adapted to suit your unique needs and circumstances.

Grief is a natural response to loss, and it's okay to permit yourself to feel it. It is vital to allow yourself to experience the full spectrum of emotions that accompany a breakup. Acknowledging your feelings without judgment is a crucial step in the healing process.

Recovering from a breakup should not be a solitary endeavor. Seeking support from friends, family, or a professional counselor is crucial when going through a breakup. Sharing your feelings and experiences with others can provide a sense of connection and alleviate feelings of isolation.

Establishing healthy boundaries is essential to the healing process. Whether it's limiting contact with your ex-partner or creating space to focus on your well-being, setting boundaries empowers you to prioritize your emotional health.

Use this time of healing as an opportunity for personal growth and self-discovery. Engage in activities that challenge and empower you. Rediscover your passions, set new goals, and invest in your development.

As you heal, shift your focus towards the future and the potential it holds. Envisioning the life you want to create for yourself and allowing hope and optimism to guide your journey can be extremely transformative during this difficult time.

The Healing Role of Self-Love

As we explore the insights shared within this section, you'll uncover how self-love acts as a beacon of light, guiding you through the darkest moments and leading you toward a path of renewed strength and empowerment.

1. Harness Self-Compassion

Instead of being your own harshest critic, treat yourself with the same kindness and understanding that you would offer a friend. Embrace your imperfections as part of your unique journey.

2. Cultivate Self-Appreciation

Recognize your strengths, accomplishments, and the qualities that make you exceptional. By focusing on your positive attributes, you will bolster your self-esteem and shift your perspective toward a more uplifting outlook.

3. Nurture Your Emotional Landscape

Self-love involves nurturing your emotional well-being. This entails acknowledging your feelings without judgment, allowing yourself to grieve, and creating a safe space for your emotions to unfold naturally.

4. Embrace Personal Growth

By nurturing a loving relationship with yourself, you create fertile ground for personal development. Embrace the opportunity to explore new passions, set goals, and continually evolve as an individual.

5. Reinvent Your Self-Image

A key aspect of self-love involves redefining your self-image. Breakups can often lead to negative self-perceptions, but by practicing self-love, you reshape how you view yourself and cultivate a positive self-concept.

6. Redefine Self-Worth

Cultivating self-love allows you to redefine your sense of self-worth. As you recognize your intrinsic value and worthiness, you'll naturally gravitate toward healthier relationships that align with your newfound understanding of your worth.

7. Forgive Yourself and Your Ex-Partner

Forgiveness is a vital component of self-love. Release any resentment or blame, both towards yourself and your ex-partner. This will allow you to unburden yourself from the weight of negativity.

8. Embrace Self-Care as a Priority

Self-love manifests through self-care practices that prioritize your physical, emotional, and mental well-being. Engage in activities that replenish your energy, elevate your mood, and reinforce the message that you deserve the best.

9. Challenge Negative Self-Talk

Abolish negative self-talk by cultivating a positive internal dialogue. Replace self-criticism with self-affirmations that reinforce your self-worth and resilience.

10. Create a Foundation for New Beginnings

Ultimately, embracing self-love creates a solid foundation for new beginnings. As you navigate your healing journey, remember that the love you invest in yourself will shape the love you attract and offer in future relationships.

Exercises for Building Self-Love and Compassion

To truly embark on a journey of healing and self-discovery after heartbreak, it's essential to actively engage in practices that cultivate self-love and compassion. This section of the book presents a collection of transformative exercises designed to empower you with the tools needed to foster a deep and unshakeable love for yourself.

Practice Daily Affirmations

One powerful way to build self-love is through daily affirmations. Creating a list of positive affirmations tailored to your needs and reciting them each day can be exceptionally powerful. By affirming your worth, you gradually shift your internal dialogue to one of positivity and self-compassion.

Write a Love Letter to Yourself

The practice of writing a heartfelt love letter to yourself can be very transformative at any time in your life when you need a little extra support. In this letter, express your admiration, appreciation, and encouragement as if you were writing to a dear friend. Be specific. Revisit this letter whenever you need a reminder of your self-worth.

Create a Self-Love Journal

Creating a self-love journal where you document your journey towards self-acceptance and self-love can help you deal with challenging negative thoughts. Use this journal to record moments of growth, achievements, and acts of self-kindness.

Practice Mindful Self-Compassion

Mindful self-compassion through meditation and mindfulness exercises can be a practical way to help you feel better about yourself. This practice involves acknowledging your emotions without judgment and offering yourself the same kindness you would extend to a friend in times of distress.

Celebrate Your Accomplishments

Celebrating your accomplishments, no matter how small they may seem, is a great way to grow your self-worth. Each achievement, no matter how minor, contributes to your journey of self-love and healing.

Reflect on Your Progress

Regularly reflect on your journey of self-love and healing. Recognize how far you've come and acknowledge the steps you've taken to prioritize your well-being.

Mindful Self Compassion

In the journey to heal from heartbreak and rebuild your sense of self, the practice of mindful self-compassion emerges as a powerful tool. This practice, rooted in mindfulness and self-kindness, enables you to embrace your emotions with a sense of understanding and gentleness. Let's explore the transformative effects of mindful self-compassion and how it can become a cornerstone of your healing process.

Cultivating Mindful Awareness

The practice of mindful self-compassion begins with cultivating mindful awareness. Mindful awareness encourages you to observe your thoughts, feelings, and bodily sensations without attempting to change or suppress them. By practicing non-judgmental observation, you create a safe space from which to explore your emotions.

The Transformative Effects

Research suggests that engaging in this practice can lead to increased well-being, reduced anxiety, and enhanced emotional regulation (Neff & Germer, 2019). By learning to approach your emotions with kindness, you create a nurturing environment for healing.

Steps to Practice Mindful Self-Compassion

> ➢ **Mindful Awareness:** Begin by tuning into your present-moment experience. Observe your thoughts, feelings, and sensations without judgment.

➤ **Self-kindness:** When facing difficulty or distress, offer yourself words of kindness and understanding. Imagine how you would comfort a dear friend in a similar situation.

➤ **Common Humanity:** Recognize that you are not alone in your suffering. Many others have experienced similar emotions and challenges.

➤ **Gentle Touch:** You can place a hand over your heart or gently touch your cheek as a physical gesture of self-soothing and compassion.

Integration Into Your Healing Journey

Mindful self-compassion can be seamlessly integrated into your daily routine. As you navigate the stages of heartbreak and healing, take moments to practice mindfulness and self-kindness. Whether it's through meditation, deep breathing, or simply offering yourself words of comfort, you'll find that the practice of mindful self-compassion provides a supportive foundation for your emotional well-being.

Avoid the Blame Trap

In the aftermath of a breakup, it's not uncommon for individuals to engage in the blame game as a way to cope with the emotional upheaval. The inclination to assign blame to the other person, or even to oneself, can be a natural response to the pain and confusion that follow a relationship's demise. However, falling into the blame trap can hinder the healing process and prolong emotional distress. Let's delve into why the blame game occurs and explore effective strategies to avoid this damaging cycle.

The phenomenon of blaming others or oneself after a breakup is a complex interplay of emotions, ego protection, and the human tendency to seek simple explanations for complex situations. This tendency often stems from a desire to make sense of the pain, frustration, and confusion that comes with the end of a relationship. Assigning blame can provide a temporary sense of relief as it shifts the focus away from the overwhelming emotional turmoil.

Recognizing the Consequences

While placing blame might provide a temporary sense of relief, it can have long-lasting negative effects on your emotional well-being and hinder your healing journey. Blaming others can perpetuate feelings of anger, resentment, and bitterness. Conversely, blaming yourself can lead to feelings of guilt, shame, and low self-esteem. These emotions can create a negative emotional cycle that prevents you from moving forward and finding closure.

Breaking the Cycle of Blame

To truly heal and grow after a breakup, it's essential to break free from the blame game. Here are some strategies to help you navigate this process:

> **Shift Perspective:** Instead of fixating on blame, shift your perspective to view the breakup as a shared experience that both individuals contributed to. Recognize that relationships are complex, and no single person is solely responsible for their outcome.

> **Practice Empathy:** Seek to understand the other person's perspective and emotions. This doesn't mean you have to agree with them, but empathizing with their feelings can promote understanding and forgiveness.

➢ **Self-Compassion:** If you find yourself blaming yourself, practice self-compassion. Treat yourself with kindness and understanding, just as you would a friend who is going through a difficult time.

➢ **Reflect and Learn:** Take time to reflect on the relationship and the breakup. Identify areas where growth and improvement are possible. Use the experience as an opportunity to learn about yourself and your needs.

➢ **Focus on Growth:** Instead of dwelling on blame, channel your energy into personal growth and self-improvement. Set goals for yourself that align with your values and aspirations.

PART 2:

YOUR HEALING GUIDE

In Part 1, we explored the intricacies of heartbreak, its emotional impact, and the stages of healing. Now, in Part 2, we shift our focus to the importance of self-love as a foundational step toward emotional recovery. We'll navigate the complexities of rebuilding your relationship with yourself, understanding the role of self-compassion, and engaging in practices that nurture your inner self.

Remember, healing takes time and patience. Embrace the process, embrace yourself, and let's dive into the world of self-love and healing together.

CHAPTER 3:
THE PSYCHOTHERAPY HEALING GUIDE

n this chapter, we will explore a powerful tool for emotional recovery: Cognitive Behavioral Therapy (CBT). As you continue on this path of healing, remember that you have the strength within you to transform your thought patterns and cultivate a healthier mindset.

In the previous sections, we delved into the emotional impact of heartbreak and the importance of self-love. Now, in Chapter 3, we shift our focus to the realm of psychotherapy, specifically CBT, which offers practical techniques to address and reframe the negative thoughts and emotions that can arise from heartbreak.

CBT – A Path to Transforming Your Thoughts

Cognitive Behavioral Therapy (CBT) is a therapeutic approach that holds immense potential for healing and personal transformation. It's a powerful tool designed to help individuals identify, challenge, and reframe negative thought patterns and behaviors that contribute to emotional distress. As we delve into the intricate workings of CBT, you'll gain a comprehensive understanding of its principles, techniques, and how it can play a pivotal role in your journey of healing from heartbreak.

At its core, CBT operates on the principle that our thoughts, feelings, behaviors, and physical sensations are interconnected. It recognizes that distorted or negative thoughts can influence our emotions and actions, ultimately affecting our overall well-being and quality of life. By targeting these thought patterns and reshaping them, CBT aims to alleviate emotional distress and promote healthier responses to life's challenges.

One of the distinguishing features of CBT is its collaborative and goal-oriented nature. In CBT sessions, you'll work closely with a trained therapist to identify specific goals you want to achieve. Whether it's managing anxiety, overcoming depression, or in our case, healing from heartbreak, CBT provides a structured framework to address these challenges methodically.

A cornerstone of CBT is recognizing and addressing cognitive distortions. These are flawed ways of thinking that can contribute to negative emotions and behaviors. Common cognitive distortions include all-or-nothing thinking, overgeneralization, magnification (catastrophizing), and emotional reasoning. Through introspection and guidance from a therapist, you'll learn to identify these distortions in your thoughts and replace them with more balanced and rational perspectives.

CBT equips you with strategies to challenge and reframe negative thought patterns. This involves examining the evidence for and against your negative thoughts, exploring alternative explanations, and considering more realistic viewpoints. By doing so, you gradually weaken the grip of distorted thinking and create space for more positive and constructive beliefs.

It's important to note that CBT is not a one-size-fits-all approach. Each individual's journey through heartbreak is unique, and CBT can be tailored to address your specific needs and challenges. As we continue exploring the intricacies of CBT in the context of healing from heartbreak, remember that your experience and progress are entirely your own. The knowledge you'll gain about CBT will empower you to embark on a transformative journey of self-discovery and emotional well-being.

How CBT Hastens Healing: A Transformative Journey to Recovery

In the aftermath of heartbreak, the emotional landscape can often feel like a tangled web of distressing thoughts and overwhelming feelings. Amidst this turbulence, CBT emerges as a beacon of hope, illuminating a transformative path towards healing. This section delves into the profound ways in which CBT expedites the healing journey, offering insights and techniques that empower individuals to transcend emotional turmoil and embrace a brighter future.

CBT's core essence lies in the restructuring of negative thought patterns, which can become deeply ingrained following heartbreak. By confronting these destructive cognitive distortions head-on, CBT assists in reshaping thought processes. This transformative process cultivates balanced, rational, and positive perspectives, effectively dispelling the clouds of negativity that often linger.

A distinctive aspect of CBT is its capacity to cultivate mindfulness and self-awareness. It equips individuals with practical techniques to observe intrusive thoughts and detach from their intense emotional grip. This newfound mindfulness empowers individuals to respond to these thoughts with detachment, reducing their impact on overall well-being and facilitating emotional regulation.

Central to CBT's philosophy is the recognition of the intricate link between thoughts and emotions. By dissecting this connection, individuals gain agency over their emotional responses. This insight can create a pivotal shift, enabling individuals to regain control over their interpretations and reactions, fostering emotional resilience.

CBT also addresses the avoidance behaviors that can develop post-heartbreak, providing tools to confront fears and build resilience. Through gradual exposure to avoided situations, individuals emerge with a sense of accomplishment and a reinforced belief in their ability to navigate challenges.

What sets CBT apart is its focus on sustainable, long-term healing. The techniques learned in therapy become a toolkit for individuals to draw upon during moments of distress. This toolbox transforms into a source of strength, enabling individuals to manage future emotional challenges effectively and promoting ongoing well-being.

The effectiveness of CBT is not mere conjecture; it is grounded in extensive scientific research and clinical success. The therapy's track record in treating various mental health issues speaks volumes about its transformative potential. Individuals embarking on the CBT journey can rest assured that they are engaging in a therapeutic approach with a proven record of fostering healing and resilience.

Utilizing CBT Techniques for Healing

As the healing journey unfolds, applying the skills garnered through CBT can become a powerful and transformative process. These skills, rooted in scientific principles, empower individuals to navigate the intricate terrain of their emotions and thoughts, offering effective tools to heal and regain emotional well-being.

One key advantage of CBT techniques is their adaptability to various scenarios. By leveraging the insights gained from therapy, individuals can effectively conceptualize and address relationship dynamics and interpersonal challenges. This empowerment enables them to break down complex problems, identify negative thought patterns, and introduce constructive alternatives.

CBT techniques extend to practical exercises that aid in coping with heartbreak. These exercises, derived from CBT principles, provide actionable steps to navigate the tumultuous emotions that often accompany breakups. By practicing mindfulness, thought restructuring, and emotional regulation, individuals can gradually dismantle the grip of distressing thoughts and emotions.

One of the foundations of CBT is recognizing the connection between thoughts, emotions, and behaviors. By actively engaging in CBT exercises, individuals learn to challenge automatic negative thoughts and replace them with rational alternatives. This process gradually shifts emotional responses, fostering resilience and emotional well-being.

CBT techniques are not limited to therapy sessions but they should be incorporated into daily life. With consistent practice, these skills become an integral part of an individual's coping arsenal. The techniques provide a toolkit that can be accessed during moments of distress, enabling individuals to manage their emotions and responses effectively.

Furthermore, CBT techniques offer a unique lens through which individuals can assess and reshape their post-breakup narratives. This reframing of thoughts encourages individuals to view challenges as opportunities for growth and transformation, further enhancing the healing process.

As with any skill, consistent practice is essential for mastery. Embracing CBT techniques requires commitment and dedication, but the rewards are profound. By cultivating self-awareness, challenging negative thoughts, and implementing healthy coping strategies, individuals can accelerate their healing journey and emerge stronger, more resilient, and better equipped to face future emotional challenges.

Identifying Negative Thought Patterns as a Consequence of Heartbreak

The aftermath of heartbreak often casts a shadow of negative thoughts that can profoundly impact an individual's emotional landscape. These thought patterns, while natural in the face of distress, can lead to a cycle of rumination and emotional turmoil. Recognizing and addressing these negative thought patterns is essential for fostering emotional healing and moving forward.

Amid the upheaval of heartbreak, common negative thought patterns can emerge. These may include dwelling on what went wrong, blaming oneself excessively, catastrophizing the future, or idealizing the past. These thought patterns can be all-encompassing, consuming an individual's mental space and perpetuating emotional distress.

Dealing with these negative thought patterns requires a multifaceted approach. One strategy is to acknowledge their presence without judgment. By recognizing that such thoughts are a natural response to a challenging situation, individuals can reduce the burden of self-criticism and create room for healing.

Engaging in self-compassion is another key aspect of addressing negative thought patterns. Treating oneself with kindness and understanding, especially during times of distress, can counteract the tendency to be overly critical. Cultivating self-compassion encourages individuals to view their pain through a lens of understanding, fostering emotional resilience.

Breaking the cycle of negative rumination involves challenging and reframing these thought patterns. This can be achieved by actively questioning the validity of these thoughts and seeking evidence to support or refute them. Often, individuals find that these negative thoughts are rooted in assumptions and distorted perceptions.

Seeking support from trusted friends, family, or professionals is an essential step in managing negative thought patterns. External perspectives can offer valuable insights and help individuals gain a more balanced view of their situation. In some cases, professional guidance may be beneficial to navigate the complexities of negative thought patterns and facilitate healing.

Challenging and Reframing Negative Thought Patterns

When grappling with the aftermath of heartbreak, negative thought patterns can become deeply ingrained, affecting one's emotional well-being and perspective. Counteracting these patterns requires a deliberate effort to challenge and reframe them, ultimately leading to a healthier mindset.

Challenging negative thought patterns involves a process of critical examination. Instead of passively accepting these thoughts as truth, individuals are encouraged to question their accuracy and validity. Often, negative thoughts are based on assumptions or distortions rather than concrete evidence. By answering probing questions, individuals can begin to unravel the underlying beliefs driving these thoughts.

Once identified, negative thoughts can be reframed through a process of cognitive restructuring. This involves replacing irrational or overly negative thoughts with more balanced and realistic alternatives. For instance, shifting from "I'm unlovable because of this breakup" to "Breakups are a natural part of life, and my worth isn't defined by this experience." This reframing process allows individuals to gain a broader perspective and consider alternative interpretations.

Implementing these strategies requires consistency and patience. Challenging and reframing negative thought patterns is an ongoing process that involves redirecting one's focus and intentionally choosing more constructive perspectives. It's important to acknowledge that change takes time and effort, but the transformation in one's emotional well-being can be profound.

Furthermore, seeking professional guidance can significantly aid in this process. CBT practitioners are skilled in assisting individuals to identify and reframe negative thought patterns. Their expertise can provide valuable insights and tailored strategies to navigate the complexities of cognitive restructuring.

Mindfulness Techniques for Healing

Mindfulness techniques offer powerful tools for navigating the challenging terrain of heartbreak, fostering emotional healing and well-being. By cultivating awareness and self-compassion, individuals can embark on a transformative journey towards healing.

Mindful Self-Compassion

This practice involves treating oneself with kindness and understanding during moments of emotional distress. Rather than harsh self-judgment, mindful self-compassion encourages individuals to acknowledge their pain without judgment. By adopting a self-compassionate stance, individuals can soothe their suffering and provide themselves with the care they need.

Mindful Meditation

Meditation can play a crucial role in healing from heartbreak. Mindful meditation involves directing one's attention to the present moment, observing thoughts and emotions without attaching judgment. This practice enhances self-awareness and helps individuals develop a healthier relationship with their thoughts. Through consistent practice, meditation can reduce the intensity of negative emotions and contribute to a greater sense of inner peace.

Breathing Exercises

Mindful breathing exercises offer a practical and accessible way to manage emotional distress. By focusing on the rhythm of their breath, individuals ground themselves in the present moment, creating a buffer between themselves and their negative thoughts. Deep, intentional breathing triggers the body's relaxation response, leading to a reduction in stress and anxiety.

Body Scan Meditation

This technique involves systematically directing attention to different parts of the body and observing sensations without judgment. Body scan meditation fosters a deeper connection between the mind and body, helping individuals become more attuned to their physical sensations. By practicing body scan meditation, individuals can alleviate tension and gain insights into the mind-body connection.

Cultivating Gratitude

Mindfulness extends beyond meditation. Cultivating gratitude involves consciously acknowledging and appreciating positive aspects of life, even in the midst of heartbreak. By shifting their focus towards the things that bring joy and comfort, individuals can counterbalance the weight of negative emotions.

Mindful Activities

Engaging in everyday activities with full presence is a form of mindfulness. Whether it's savoring a meal, taking a walk, or engaging in creative pursuits, dedicating one's attention to the activity at hand fosters a sense of grounding and provides a respite from intrusive thoughts.

Utilizing CBT Worksheets for Healing

CBT worksheets offer practical exercises to navigate the challenging journey of healing after heartbreak. These worksheets are designed to help individuals identify negative thought patterns, reframe unhelpful beliefs, and cultivate healthier coping strategies.

Thought Record Worksheets

Thought records are a fundamental tool in CBT. These worksheets guide individuals to identify and analyze their thoughts, emotions, and resulting behaviors. By breaking down negative thought patterns, individuals can challenge distorted thinking and develop more balanced perspectives.

Example worksheet:

Situation: Describe the situation that triggered your negative thoughts

---

Emotion: Identify the main emotion you felt during this situation.

Automatic Thought: Write down the thought that came to your mind in response to the situation. Be specific and concise.

Evidence For: List any evidence or reasons that support the automatic thought.

Evidence Against: Identify any evidence or reasons that contradict or challenge the automatic thought.

Alternative Thought: Generate a more balanced and rational thought that takes into account the evidence against the automatic thought.

Emotion (Revised): Reevaluate your emotion after considering the alternative thought. Rate the intensity of the emotion on a scale from 0 to 10.

Resulting Behavior: Describe how the automatic thought influenced your behavior or actions in response to the situation.

Outcome: Reflect on how the situation turned out and whether your initial automatic thought accurately predicted the outcome.

Learning Point: What have you learned from this exercise? How has it helped you gain a more balanced perspective?

Practice: Consider a similar situation in the future where you can apply the skills you've learned from this thought record. Write down how you would approach it differently, using more balanced thinking.

Optional: Share this thought record with a therapist or trusted friend for additional insights and feedback.

Remember, the goal of this thought record is to help you become more aware of your automatic thoughts, challenge negative patterns, and develop healthier ways of thinking. With practice, you can gain control over your thoughts and emotions, leading to more balanced and adaptive responses to challenging situations.

Belief Restructuring Worksheets

These worksheets focus on identifying and addressing core beliefs that contribute to negative emotions. By examining these deep-seated beliefs and replacing them with more realistic alternatives, individuals can reshape their outlook on the breakup and their self-worth.

Example worksheet:

Core Belief: Identify the core belief that you hold about yourself, relationships, or the breakup. Be honest and specific.

Emotion Associated: Write down the primary emotion that arises when you think about or hold onto this core belief.

Evidence Supporting Core Belief: List instances or experiences from your past that seem to support this core belief. Be as objective as possible.

_____

_____

_____

_____

Evidence Challenging Core Belief: Identify any experiences, examples, or counterarguments that contradict or challenge this core belief.

_____

_____

_____

_____

Alternative Belief: Formulate a more balanced and realistic alternative belief that takes into account the evidence against the core belief.

_____

_____

_____

_____

Emotion Associated (Revised): Reevaluate the emotion associated with the core belief after considering the alternative belief. Rate the intensity of the emotion on a scale from 0 to 10.

_____

Impact of Core Belief: Reflect on how this core belief has impacted your thoughts, feelings, and behaviors following the breakup.

_____

_____

_____

_____

New Perspective: Consider how adopting the alternative belief could change your outlook on the breakup, yourself, and future relationships.

_____

_____

_____

_____

Action Steps: Write down actionable steps you can take to reinforce the new perspective and challenge the old core belief when it arises.

_____

_____

_____

_____

Practice: Choose a situation in which your old core belief might have influenced your thoughts and actions. Describe how you can respond differently based on the new perspective.

_____

_____

_____

_____

Optional: Share your core belief, alternative belief, and action steps with a therapist or supportive friend for feedback and guidance.

_____

_____

_____

_____

The purpose of this belief restructuring worksheet is to help you identify and modify deep-seated core beliefs that contribute to negative emotions. By challenging and replacing these beliefs, you can shift your emotional responses, improve your self-worth, and foster a healthier outlook on breakups and future relationships.

Activity Scheduling Worksheets

Heartbreak often leads to a decrease in engagement with enjoyable activities. Activity scheduling worksheets encourage individuals to plan and engage in activities that bring joy and a sense of accomplishment. This practice helps counteract feelings of sadness and isolation.

Example worksheet:

Date: Choose a specific date for the activity schedule.

Time: Decide on a suitable time for each activity.

Activity: List the activity you plan to engage in. It can be something you used to enjoy or something new you'd like to try.

Location: Specify where you will carry out the activity.

Duration: Estimate how long you intend to spend on this activity.

Goal: Identify what you hope to achieve or experience through this activity.

Emotion Before: Rate your current emotional state before engaging in the activity on a scale from 0 to 10 (0 being extremely sad, 10 being very positive).

Thoughts Before: Write down any thoughts or concerns you have before starting the activity.

_____

_____

_____

_____

Emotion After: Rate your emotional state after completing the activity on a scale from 0 to 10.

_____

Thoughts After: Reflect on how your thoughts have changed or evolved after engaging in the activity.

_____

_____

_____

_____

Achievement: Consider whether you achieved the goal you set for this activity.

_____

_____

_____

_____

Notes: Use this space to jot down any observations, surprises, or insights that emerged during or after the activity.

_____

_____

_____

_____

Next Activity: Plan the next activity you'd like to engage in, considering what you've learned from this experience.

_____

Optional: Share your activity schedule and reflections with a therapist or friend for accountability and support.

_____

_____

_____

_____

The purpose of this activity scheduling worksheet is to encourage you to engage in enjoyable and meaningful activities to counteract feelings of sadness and isolation. By planning and participating in these activities, you can experience positive emotions, a sense of accomplishment, and gradually improve your overall well-being during the healing process.

Gratitude Journal Worksheets

Practicing gratitude is an effective way to shift focus from negative emotions to positive aspects of life. Gratitude journal worksheets guide individuals to reflect on daily moments of gratitude, fostering a more optimistic perspective.

Example worksheet:

Date: Record the date for the day you're writing in your gratitude journal.

Morning/Evening: Decide whether you'll reflect on moments of gratitude in the morning or evening.

Three Things I'm Grateful For:

1. Write down the first thing you're grateful for and why.

   ---

2. Write down the second thing you're grateful for and why.

   ---

3. Write down the third thing you're grateful for and why.

Positive Emotions: Reflect on how expressing gratitude makes you feel. Did it uplift your mood or shift your perspective?

Impact: Consider how focusing on gratitude affects your overall outlook for the day.

_____

_____

_____

Optional: Include any additional thoughts, insights, or experiences related to gratitude.

_____

_____

_____

Next Day: Anticipate something you're looking forward to tomorrow. This can be another opportunity for gratitude.

_____

_____

_____

Overall Reflection: Take a moment to reflect on how maintaining a gratitude journal is impacting your daily life and emotional well-being.

_____

_____

_____

The purpose of this gratitude journal worksheet is to encourage you to focus on the positive aspects of your life and cultivate a more optimistic perspective. By regularly recording moments of gratitude, you can shift your attention away from negative emotions and enhance your overall sense of well-being during the healing process.

Coping Strategy Worksheets

Coping strategy worksheets help individuals compile a personalized toolbox of healthy coping skills. From deep breathing exercises to engaging in hobbies, these worksheets encourage the exploration and practice of various coping techniques.

Example worksheet:

Date: Record the date for the day you're creating your coping strategy worksheet.

_____

Emotional State: Identify your current emotional state (e.g., sad, anxious, stressed, etc.).

_____

Trigger: Describe the situation or event that triggered this emotional state.

_____

_____

_____

_____

Healthy Coping Strategies: List at least five healthy coping strategies you can use to manage your emotions more positively.

1. **Deep Breathing:** Practice deep breathing exercises to calm your mind and body.

   _____

2. **Journaling:** Write down your thoughts and feelings to gain clarity and release emotional tension.

   _____

3. **Physical Activity:** Engage in a workout, walk, or yoga session to release endorphins and reduce stress.

   _____

4. **Mindfulness Meditation:** Practice mindfulness to stay present and reduce emotional reactivity.

   _____

5. **Listening to Music:** Choose music that matches your mood to help you process and express your emotions.

   _____

Implementing Coping Strategies: Choose one or more coping strategies from the list above to implement today.

1. **Strategy:** Select a coping strategy you'd like to use.

   _____

   _____

   _____

   _____

2. **How You'll Implement:** Describe how you will apply this strategy in your current situation.

_____

_____

_____

_____

3. **Expected Outcome:** Predict how using this coping strategy might affect your emotional state.

_____

_____

_____

_____

Reflection: After implementing the chosen coping strategy, reflect on how it helped you manage your emotions. Did it provide relief, shift your perspective, or help you navigate the situation more effectively?

_____

_____

_____

_____

Adding to Your Toolbox: Think of other healthy coping strategies you'd like to add to your toolbox. Write them down so you can refer to them in the future.

_____

_____

_____

_____

By completing this coping strategy worksheet, you're building a collection of effective tools to manage your emotions during challenging times. Regularly practicing these strategies can enhance your ability to cope with heartbreak and navigate various emotional experiences.

Goal Setting Worksheets

Setting achievable goals post-heartbreak can provide a sense of direction and purpose. Goal-setting worksheets assist individuals in defining realistic goals that contribute to their overall well-being and personal growth.

Example worksheet:

Date: Record the date for the day you're creating your goal-setting worksheet.

_____

Emotional State: Describe your current emotional state after the heartbreak (e.g., sadness, confusion, etc.).

_____

Long-Term Vision: Imagine yourself several months from now. How do you want to feel emotionally, mentally, and physically? What kind of person do you aspire to become as you heal from the heartbreak?

_____

_____

_____

_____

SMART Goals: Set SMART goals (Specific, Measurable, Achievable, Relevant, and Time-bound) that align with your long-term vision and promote your well-being. Write down at least three goals.

1. Goal: State your first SMART goal.

> **Specific:** Clearly describe what you want to achieve.

_____

> **Measurable:** Include a way to measure your progress.

_____

> **Achievable:** Ensure the goal is realistic and attainable.

_____

> **Relevant:** Confirm that the goal is meaningful to your healing journey.

_____

➢ **Time-bound:** Set a deadline for achieving the goal.

_____

➢ **Plan:** Outline the steps or actions you'll take to reach this goal.

_____

➢ **Obstacles:** Identify potential challenges and how you'll overcome them.

_____

➢ **Support:** List any resources or support systems you'll utilize.

_____

2. Goal: State your second SMART goal using the same format as above.

_____

_____

_____

_____

3. Goal: State your third SMART goal using the same format as above.

_____

_____

_____

_____

Visualizing Success: Imagine yourself achieving these goals. How would it feel? How would it impact your overall well-being and healing process?

Next Steps: Review your SMART goals and action plans regularly. Track your progress and adjust your goals as needed. Remember that healing is a journey, and achieving these goals is a positive step forward.

By engaging with these CBT worksheets, individuals can actively participate in their healing process. The structured exercises offer a way to process emotions, challenge negative thoughts, and develop effective coping strategies. While healing from heartbreak is a complex journey, these practical tools provide individuals with a sense of agency and empowerment as they work toward emotional well-being.

CHAPTER 4:
HEALING FROM TRAUMA

Dealing with heartbreak can have profound effects on our mental and emotional well-being. For some, the aftermath of heartbreak can lead to mental health challenges and a sense of emotional upheaval. In this chapter, we delve into the intricate world of healing from trauma brought about by heartbreak. Recognizing that the journey to recovery is unique for each individual, this chapter offers insights and strategies to guide you toward restoring your mental health.

The Mental Health Implications

The aftermath of heartbreak can cast a significant shadow on one's mental health, triggering a range of emotional responses and cognitive shifts that can lead to distressing mental states. This section delves into the profound mental health implications that heartbreak can have on individuals, shedding light on the intricacies of these challenges and offering insights into how they affect our emotional and psychological well-being.

Emotional Turmoil and Psychological Distress

Heartbreak often ushers in a period of emotional turmoil. Feelings of sadness, grief, anger, and confusion can overwhelm individuals as they navigate the aftermath of a severed emotional bond. The intensity of these emotions can lead to emotional exhaustion, increased stress, and a heightened sense of vulnerability. Such emotional distress might manifest as sleep disturbances, appetite changes, and a general sense of heaviness and unease.

Impact on Cognitive Function

Heartbreak can significantly impact cognitive function, leading to difficulties in concentration, decision-making, and memory. Individuals may find it challenging to focus on daily tasks or make clear-headed decisions due to the emotional turbulence that accompanies heartbreak. Constant rumination on the relationship, its ending, and what could have been can further hinder cognitive abilities.

Increased Risk of Mental Health Conditions

The emotional upheaval caused by heartbreak can also increase the vulnerability to mental health conditions. Conditions such as depression and anxiety are common companions of heartbreak, as the experience of loss and emotional upheaval can disrupt the brain's natural chemistry. These conditions may manifest as persistent feelings of sadness, hopelessness, and excessive worry.

Changes in Brain Activity

Recent research has unveiled the neurological impacts of heartbreak. Neuroimaging studies have shown that areas of the brain associated with reward processing, attachment, and emotional regulation can undergo changes in response to heartbreak. This can result in altered brain activity patterns that contribute to emotional dysregulation and the perpetuation of negative thought patterns (Winch, 2018).

Navigating these mental health implications necessitates a combination of self-awareness, self-care, and, when needed, professional support. Understanding that these challenges are a natural response to significant emotional upheaval can be the first step toward acknowledging the need for healing.

Trauma and the Fight or Flight Response

The human response to trauma is complex, often involving a cascade of physiological and psychological reactions designed to ensure survival in the face of danger. One such response is the well-known "fight or flight" mechanism, which is intricately linked to the body's stress response system. This section delves into the profound effects of trauma on the "fight or flight" response, exploring how it manifests and interacts with the emotional aftermath of heartbreak.

The Flight Trauma Response

The flight trauma response involves a visceral urge to escape or distance oneself from the source of danger. This response can manifest both physically and emotionally. Individuals experiencing the flight response may feel overwhelmed by a compelling need to flee from situations, places, or even emotions associated with the traumatic experience. This might manifest as avoiding reminders of the heartbreak, seeking distractions, or withdrawing from social interactions to minimize emotional discomfort.

The Fight Trauma Response

Conversely, the fight response activates an instinct to confront the threat head-on. While this response is essential for survival in acute danger, it can manifest as heightened aggression, irritability, or a tendency to engage in conflicts or arguments. Individuals might find themselves emotionally charged and reactive, battling against their feelings of pain and loss through a confrontational approach.

The Freeze, Fawn, and Flop Responses

Beyond fight and flight, trauma can evoke other responses like freeze, fawn, and flop. The freeze response entails a sense of immobilization or feeling stuck, unable to move forward. The fawn response involves adapting to the trauma by seeking to please or appease others, often at the expense of one's own needs. The flop response, on the other hand, is characterized by a sense of defeat and surrender, leading to feelings of hopelessness and helplessness.

Interaction With Heartbreak

Heartbreak, being a form of emotional trauma, can activate these trauma responses, leading to a complex interplay between survival instincts and emotional healing. For instance, an individual may feel an intense desire to avoid emotional pain (flight) while simultaneously experiencing moments of anger or confrontation (fight) when confronting reminders of the lost relationship. The freeze, fawn, and flop responses can also influence how individuals cope with the emotional aftermath of heartbreak.

Understanding how trauma and the "fight or flight" response intersect can offer insights into the range of emotions and reactions individuals may experience after heartbreak. Recognizing these responses and their implications can guide individuals toward seeking appropriate support, developing coping strategies, and ultimately embarking on a healing journey that addresses the multifaceted impact of trauma on mental well-being.

Healthy Coping Mechanisms

Navigating the complex emotional landscape following heartbreak requires effective coping mechanisms that promote healing and well-being. These mechanisms serve as tools to manage distress, build resilience, and gradually restore a sense of emotional equilibrium. Here, we delve into various healthy coping strategies that individuals can employ to support their recovery journey after experiencing heartbreak.

Mindfulness and Meditation

Engaging in mindfulness practices and meditation can provide a refuge for individuals to observe their thoughts and emotions without judgment. These techniques foster self-awareness, enhance emotional regulation, and offer a space to process feelings associated with heartbreak.

Physical Activity

Regular physical exercise has proven benefits for mental health. Engaging in physical activity, whether it's jogging, yoga, or dancing, releases endorphins that help elevate mood, reduce stress, and contribute to overall well-being.

Journaling and Expressive Writing

Writing down thoughts, feelings, and experiences related to heartbreak can be a cathartic process. Journaling offers a safe outlet to express emotions, gain insights into one's feelings, and track personal growth over time.

Seeking Social Support

Connecting with friends, family, or support groups provides opportunities to share feelings and receive empathy. Social interactions help individuals feel understood, validated, and less isolated on their journey.

Creative Expression

Engaging in creative activities such as art, music, or writing can serve as a channel for emotional expression and processing. Creative endeavors offer an avenue to transform pain into meaningful and constructive outputs.

Healthy Lifestyle Choices

Nurturing the body with proper nutrition, adequate sleep, and hydration contributes to emotional well-being. A balanced lifestyle supports cognitive function and emotional resilience.

Seeking Professional Help

Therapeutic interventions, such as individual counseling or group therapy, can provide structured support tailored to one's needs. Mental health professionals offer guidance in processing emotions, developing coping strategies, and fostering personal growth.

These healthy coping mechanisms can be combined and adapted to suit an individual's preferences and needs. By incorporating these strategies into their healing journey, individuals can effectively navigate the emotional aftermath of heartbreak, promote resilience, and lay the foundation for future emotional well-being.

5 Effective Strategies for Healing

Navigating the path to healing after experiencing heartbreak is a unique and personal journey. While the emotional impact may vary from person to person, there are several effective strategies that individuals can employ to support their healing process. These strategies, drawn from various sources, offer insights and guidance for those seeking to mend their hearts and restore their well-being.

Practicing Self-Compassion

Treating oneself with kindness and understanding during times of heartbreak is crucial. Acknowledging pain without self-judgment and offering the same compassion one would extend to a friend fosters emotional healing. Self-compassion allows individuals to navigate their emotions with gentleness and patience.

Engaging in Self-Care Rituals

Prioritizing self-care by engaging in activities that promote well-being can provide solace during challenging times. Whether it's taking long walks, enjoying a soothing bath, practicing meditation, or indulging in hobbies, self-care rituals offer moments of respite and rejuvenation.

Seeking Professional Support

Reaching out to mental health professionals, such as therapists or counselors, can provide invaluable guidance and support. Professionals equipped with therapeutic tools can help individuals process their emotions, develop coping strategies, and gain insights into their healing journey.

Focusing on Personal Growth

Heartbreak can be an opportunity for personal growth and self-discovery. Exploring new interests, setting goals, and working toward self-improvement can help individuals shift their focus from the pain of the past to the possibilities of the future.

Cultivating a Supportive Network

Surrounding oneself with friends, family, and a supportive community can alleviate feelings of isolation and loneliness. Sharing experiences, seeking advice, and receiving empathy from loved ones can provide emotional validation and a sense of belonging.

These effective strategies for healing are not linear; individuals may find that certain approaches resonate more with them than others. The healing journey is marked by ups and downs, progress, and setbacks. By incorporating these strategies into their daily lives, individuals can gradually mend their hearts, find resilience, and pave the way for a brighter emotional future.

Choosing Psychotherapy: Which Is Best?

When it comes to healing from heartbreak, psychotherapy can be a powerful ally on the path to emotional recovery. The decision to seek therapy can be transformative, but with various therapeutic approaches available, how does one choose the most suitable option? Here, we explore different psychotherapy methods and considerations to help individuals make an informed choice in their healing journey.

Traditional Talk Therapy

Traditional talk therapy, also known as "psychoanalytic" or "psychodynamic therapy," delves into past experiences, exploring how they may influence present emotions and behaviors. It aims to uncover unconscious patterns and unresolved conflicts that may contribute to emotional struggles, making it a valuable choice for those seeking deeper insights into their heartbreak's roots.

Cognitive-Behavioral Therapy (CBT)

CBT is renowned for its structured approach to addressing negative thought patterns and behaviors. It focuses on challenging distorted thoughts, developing coping skills, and promoting positive behavioral changes. CBT is ideal for individuals looking to reframe their thinking and adopt healthier responses to heartbreak-related distress.

Mindfulness-Based Therapy

Mindfulness-based therapies emphasize being present in the moment and observing thoughts and emotions without judgment. Mindfulness techniques can help individuals manage overwhelming emotions, reduce rumination, and foster self-compassion, which is particularly beneficial for those seeking a more balanced perspective after heartbreak.

Interpersonal Therapy

Interpersonal therapy centers around relationships and communication patterns. It addresses how heartbreak can impact one's interactions with others, providing tools to navigate challenges and develop healthier relationship dynamics. This approach suits individuals aiming to improve their relational skills and connections.

Integrative or Eclectic Therapy

Some therapists combine elements from various therapeutic approaches to create a personalized treatment plan. Integrative therapy can be especially effective for those seeking a tailored approach that addresses their unique needs and preferences.

Choosing the right psychotherapy approach involves considering personal preferences, treatment goals, and the therapist's expertise. It's essential to consult with a mental health professional who can assess individual needs and recommend the most suitable therapy for healing. Keep in mind that therapy is a collaborative process, and the therapeutic relationship between the client and therapist plays a vital role in the overall success of the healing journey.

The Power of Forgiveness

Navigating the aftermath of heartbreak often involves grappling with feelings of hurt, anger, and resentment. While these emotions are natural responses, embracing the power of forgiveness can be a transformative step toward healing. Forgiveness isn't about condoning hurtful actions or minimizing pain; rather, it's a personal choice to release the emotional burden that may keep one tethered to the past. Here, we delve into the significance of forgiveness in the healing process and how it can contribute to emotional well-being.

Emotional Liberation

Forgiveness is a powerful act of emotional liberation. When we hold onto anger and resentment, we inadvertently give power to the person or situation that hurt us. Choosing forgiveness allows us to reclaim our emotional autonomy, releasing ourselves from the grip of negative emotions that can hinder healing.

Breaking the Cycle

Unresolved pain and resentment can create a cycle of negative emotions that affect future relationships and experiences. Forgiveness breaks this cycle, freeing us from the pattern of reliving the hurt. By letting go of past grievances, we create space for new and positive experiences to unfold.

Self-Healing

Forgiveness is a gift to oneself. It's an acknowledgment that our well-being is a priority, and holding onto anger can have detrimental effects on our mental and even physical health. By forgiving, we initiate a process of self-healing, fostering inner peace and emotional resilience.

Empowerment

Forgiveness is an empowering choice that allows us to reclaim control over our emotions and reactions. Instead of being consumed by anger or resentment, we decide to channel our energy into self-improvement and growth. This empowerment contributes to building a stronger sense of self and confidence.

Opening to Love and Trust

Releasing the weight of resentment can make room for love, trust, and healthy new relationships. When we forgive, we free ourselves from carrying emotional baggage into future connections, fostering an environment of openness and vulnerability.

Cultivating Compassion

Forgiveness often involves cultivating compassion, both for ourselves and the person who hurt us. Recognizing that everyone has struggles and flaws helps us see the bigger picture and view the situation with greater understanding.

Forgiveness is a process that takes time and self-reflection. It's not always easy, and it doesn't necessarily mean reconciling with the person who caused the pain. Instead, it's about finding peace within ourselves and moving forward without being burdened by past wounds. While forgiveness may not erase the hurt, it can significantly lighten the emotional load and contribute to the overall healing journey.

CBT Worksheets for Healing

CBT provides a structured and effective framework for healing from emotional wounds, such as those caused by heartbreak. Integrating CBT worksheets into your healing journey can facilitate self-awareness, challenge negative thought patterns, and promote healthier coping strategies. These worksheets offer valuable tools to navigate the complex emotions that often accompany a breakup, aiding in the process of rebuilding and healing. Here are some CBT worksheets that can benefit your healing process:

Thought Record Worksheets

These worksheets guide you in identifying, analyzing, and reframing negative thoughts that contribute to emotional distress. By breaking down negative thought patterns, you can challenge distorted thinking and develop more balanced perspectives on the breakup.

Example:

Situation: After the breakup, I saw my ex-partner at a social event talking and laughing with someone else.

Emotion: Overwhelming sadness and jealousy.

Automatic Thought: "They're so happy without me. I must have been a terrible partner."

Evidence Supporting This Thought:

- They are laughing and seem to be having a good time.
- They didn't seem upset after the breakup.
- I've been feeling lonely since the breakup.

Evidence Against This Thought:

- People often pretend to be okay, even if they're not.
- My ex-partner's emotions might not be as simple as they appear.
- I've had happy moments without them, too.

Alternative Thought: "It's natural for them to socialize and have fun. Our relationship had its ups and downs, and their current demeanor doesn't define my worth."

Emotion After Considering Alternative Thoughts: Still some sadness, but it is less intense and more balanced.

Re-rate Emotion: 6/10 (down from 9/10)

Action Plan: Instead of dwelling on their interactions, I'll focus on enjoying the event and connecting with friends. I'll remind myself that my worth is not determined by their behavior.

Example for you to fill out:

Situation:

_____

_____

_____

Emotion:

_____

Automatic Thought:

_____

_____

_____

Evidence Supporting This Thought:

_____

_____

_____

Evidence Against This Thought:

_____

_____

_____

Alternative Thought:

_____

_____

_____

Emotion After Considering Alternative Thought:

_____

_____

_____

Re-rate Emotion:

_____

Action Plan:

_____

_____

_____

Belief Restructuring Worksheets

These worksheets focus on addressing deep-seated beliefs that contribute to negative emotions. By examining and replacing these core beliefs with more realistic alternatives, you can reshape your outlook on the breakup and your self-worth.

Example:

Negative Core Belief: "I'm unlovable and destined to be alone."

Origins of Belief: Growing up, I faced rejection and felt excluded by peers.

Emotions Linked to Belief: Low self-esteem, fear of abandonment, and sadness.

Challenging Belief:

> ➢ Identify Evidence Against the Belief: I've had meaningful relationships in the past where I felt loved and valued.

> ➢ Consider Alternative Explanations: My past experiences might not accurately predict my future relationships.

➢ Explore Counterexamples: There have been moments when friends and family have shown me love and support.

➢ Question the Validity: Is it fair to generalize my worth based on a few negative experiences?

Constructing a Balanced Belief: "I am capable of forming meaningful connections. My worth isn't determined by past rejections, and I have the power to create positive relationships in the future."

Emotions After Restructuring: Empowerment, hope, and increased self-compassion.

Example for you to fill out:
Negative Core Belief:

Origins of Belief:

Emotions Linked to Belief:

Challenging Belief:

> Identify Evidence Against the Belief:

_____

> Consider Alternative Explanations:

_____

> Explore Counterexamples:

_____

> Question the Validity:

_____

Constructing a Balanced Belief:

_____

_____

_____

Emotions After Restructuring:

_____

Activity Scheduling Worksheets

Heartbreak often leads to decreased engagement with enjoyable activities. These worksheets encourage you to plan and engage in activities that bring joy and a sense of accomplishment, countering feelings of sadness and isolation.

Example:

Date: [Insert Date]

Goals for the Week:

> ➤ To engage in activities that bring joy and a sense of accomplishment
> ➤ To counter feelings of sadness and isolation

List of Activities:

Monday:

> ➤ Morning: 30-minute walk in the park
> ➤ Afternoon: Call a friend and plan a virtual game night

Tuesday:

> ➤ Morning: 20-minute yoga session at home
> ➤ Afternoon: Try a new recipe and cook a homemade dinner

Wednesday:

> ➤ Morning: Listen to a podcast during breakfast
> ➤ Afternoon: Attend a virtual art workshop

Thursday:

> ➤ Morning: Write in a gratitude journal
> ➤ Afternoon: Watch a movie that makes me laugh

Friday:

> ➤ Morning: Explore a new hiking trail
> ➤ Afternoon: Have a video call with a family member

Saturday:

> ➢ Morning: Meditate for 15 minutes
> ➢ Afternoon: Start reading a new book

Sunday:

> ➢ Morning: Visit a local museum or art gallery
> ➢ Afternoon: Work on a creative project

Additional Notes:

> ➢ Focus on being present and fully engaged in each activity.
> ➢ Don't hesitate to adjust the schedule if unexpected opportunities arise.
> ➢ Remember that engaging in enjoyable activities can have a positive impact on my mood and overall well-being.

Example for you to fill out:

Date:

_____

Goals for the Week:

> ➢ _____
> ➢ _____

List of Activities:

Monday:

> ➢ Morning: _____
> ➢ Afternon: _____

Tuesday:

> ➤ Morning: _____

> ➤ Afternon: _____

Wednesday:

> ➤ Morning: _____

> ➤ Afternon: _____

Thursday:

> ➤ Morning: _____

> ➤ Afternon: _____

Friday:

> ➤ Morning: _____

> ➤ Afternon: _____

Saturday:

> ➤ Morning: _____

> ➤ Afternon: _____

Sunday:

> ➤ Morning: _____

> ➤ Afternon: _____

Additional Notes:

> ➤ _____
>
> _____

➢ _____

_____

➢ _____

_____

Gratitude Journal Worksheets

Practicing gratitude can shift your focus from negative emotions to positive aspects of life. Gratitude journal worksheets guide you to reflect on daily moments of gratitude, fostering a more optimistic perspective.

Date: [Insert Date]

Things I'm Grateful for Today:

➢ **Morning Sunshine:** I woke up to a bright and sunny day, which lifted my spirits right away.

➢ **Supportive Friends:** Received a heartfelt message from a friend, reminding me of the strong connections in my life.

➢ **Warm Cup of Tea:** Enjoyed a peaceful moment with a cup of my favorite tea, allowing myself to savor the simple pleasures.

➢ **Nature's Beauty:** Took a walk in the park and appreciated the beauty of blooming flowers and singing birds.

➢ **Cozy Reading Nook:** Spent some time immersed in a book in my cozy reading corner, finding solace in a captivating story.

➢ **Delicious Lunch:** Prepared and relished a delicious and nourishing homemade lunch that filled me with gratitude for good food.

- ➤ **Phone Call with Family:** Had a heartwarming conversation with a family member, feeling grateful for the love and connection.

- ➤ **Opportunities Ahead:** Reflected on upcoming projects and plans, feeling excited about the possibilities the future holds.

Daily Affirmation: "I am cultivating a mindset of gratitude, finding joy in the little moments that make life beautiful."

Reflection: Taking time each day to acknowledge the things I'm grateful for has helped me shift my focus from negative emotions to positive aspects of life. This gratitude journaling practice allows me to nurture an optimistic perspective and appreciate the abundance of goodness that surrounds me.

Example for you to fill out:

Date: _____

Things I'm Grateful for Today:

- ➤ _____

_____

- ➤ _____

_____

- ➤ _____

_____

➢ _____

_____

➢ _____

_____

Daily Affirmation:

_____

_____

Reflection:

_____

_____

_____

_____

Coping Strategy Worksheets

These worksheets help you compile a personalized toolbox of healthy coping skills. From deep breathing exercises to engaging in hobbies, these worksheets encourage exploration and practice of various coping techniques.

Date: [Insert Date]

Challenging Situation: Feeling overwhelmed by post-breakup emotions and longing for a sense of calm.

Healthy Coping Strategies:

- ➢ **Deep Breathing:** Practice deep breathing exercises to instantly ground myself and reduce anxiety. Inhale for a count of four, hold for four, and exhale for four.

- ➢ **Mindful Meditation:** Set aside 10 minutes for mindfulness meditation, focusing on my breath and allowing thoughts to come and go without judgment.

- ➢ **Engage in Creative Outlet:** Spend time painting or drawing to express my emotions and channel my energy into a creative activity.

- ➢ **Physical Activity:** Go for a brisk walk or jog to release endorphins and boost my mood while benefiting from the positive effects of exercise.

- ➢ **Journaling:** Write in my journal to articulate my feelings and thoughts, gaining clarity and a sense of release through self-expression.

- ➢ **Listening to Uplifting Music:** Create a playlist of songs that resonate with my emotions and uplift my spirits, providing comfort and connection.

- ➢ **Reaching Out to a Friend:** Connect with a supportive friend, either through a call or message, to share my feelings and receive reassurance.

- ➢ **Engaging in a Hobby:** Spend time on a favorite hobby, such as cooking, gardening, or playing a musical instrument, to find joy and distraction.

> **Visualization:** Close my eyes and visualize a peaceful place, like a beach or a forest, to mentally escape and find tranquility.

> **Positive Self-Affirmations:** Repeat positive affirmations, such as "I am resilient and capable of healing," to cultivate self-confidence and inner strength.

Action Plan: I will keep this worksheet handy and choose at least two coping strategies from my toolbox whenever I face challenging emotions. By practicing these techniques, I can better manage my emotions and work towards healing and resilience.

Reflection: Creating a personalized list of coping strategies has empowered me to navigate difficult emotions healthily. These tools provide a sense of control and empowerment, helping me cope with the ups and downs of post-breakup life.

Example for you to fill out:

Date: _____

Challenging Situation:

_____

_____

Healthy Coping Strategies:

> _____

_____

➢ _____

_____

➢ _____

_____

➢ _____

_____

➢ _____

_____

➢ _____

_____

➢ _____

_____

➢ _____

_____

➢ _____

_____

➢ _____

_____

Action Plan:

_____

_____

_____

Reflection:

_____

_____

_____

Goal-Setting Worksheets

Setting achievable goals post-heartbreak can provide a sense of direction and purpose. Goal-setting worksheets assist you in defining realistic goals that contribute to your overall well-being and personal growth.

Date: [Insert Date]

Current State: Feeling emotionally drained after a breakup, seeking to regain a sense of purpose and personal growth.

Long-Term Goal: To rebuild my self-esteem, find new passions, and create a fulfilling life post-heartbreak.

Short-Term Goals:

> ➤ **Physical Health:** Engage in regular exercise three times a week to improve my physical well-being and boost my mood.

> ➤ **Self-Care Ritual:** Dedicate 15 minutes each morning to mindfulness meditation to start the day with a clear mind and positive intention.

➢ **Social Connection:** Reconnect with friends and initiate plans to meet up at least once a week to foster a strong support network.

➢ **New Skill Acquisition:** Enroll in a photography class to explore a creative outlet and gain a new skill that sparks joy.

➢ **Career Development:** Update my resume and apply for at least three new job opportunities that align with my career aspirations.

➢ **Hobby Revival:** Devote time every weekend to playing the piano, reigniting my love for music, and finding solace in the familiar melodies.

➢ **Journaling Practice:** Write in my gratitude journal every evening to cultivate a positive mindset and acknowledge daily blessings.

➢ **Volunteer Work:** Research local volunteer opportunities and commit to contributing my time to a cause I'm passionate about.

➢ **Healthy Lifestyle:** Incorporate more fruits and vegetables into my diet and prioritize getting adequate sleep each night.

➢ **Positive Affirmations:** Develop a list of affirmations that promote self-love and resilience, reciting them daily for a confident mindset.

Plan of Action:

➢ For each short-term goal, I will create a specific plan with actionable steps and deadlines.

➢ I will track my progress regularly and celebrate small achievements along the way.

➢ I will adjust goals if needed, considering any changes in circumstances or preferences.

Reflection: Setting these goals has given me a renewed sense of purpose and direction. By focusing on my well-being and personal growth, I'm building a foundation for a brighter future post-heartbreak.

Example for you to fill out:

Goal-Setting Worksheets

Setting achievable goals post-heartbreak can provide a sense of direction and purpose. Goal-setting worksheets assist you in defining realistic goals that contribute to your overall well-being and personal growth.

Date: _____

Current State:

_____

_____

Long-Term Goal:

_____

_____

_____

Short-Term Goals:

➢ _____

   _____

➢ _____

_____

➢ _____

_____

➢ _____

_____

➢ _____

_____

➢ _____

_____

➢ _____

_____

➢ _____

_____

➢ _____

_____

➢ _____

_____

Plan of Action:

➤ _____

_____

➤ _____

_____

➤ _____

_____

Reflection:

_____

_____

_____

_____

_____

_____

Integrating these CBT worksheets into your healing process can enhance your self-understanding, emotional regulation, and overall resilience. They offer a structured approach to challenging negative thought patterns, promoting self-compassion, and fostering positive changes in your emotional well-being. While these worksheets provide a framework, remember that your healing journey is unique, and it's important to tailor these tools to your individual needs and preferences.

Mindfulness Meditation Techniques

Mindfulness meditation is a powerful practice that can help you manage the emotional aftermath of heartbreak. It involves being fully present in the moment and observing your thoughts and feelings without judgment. Here are some effective mindfulness meditation techniques to incorporate into your healing journey:

Breath Awareness Meditation

Find a quiet and comfortable space to sit or lie down. Close your eyes and focus your attention on your breath. Notice the sensation of your breath as you inhale and exhale. If your mind wanders, gently bring your focus back to your breath.

Example: Inhale deeply for a count of four, hold for four counts, and exhale for four counts. Repeat this cycle.

Body Scan Meditation

Lie down in a comfortable position and close your eyes. Start from your toes and slowly move your attention upward through each part of your body. Notice any sensations, tension, or discomfort.

Example: As you focus on each body part, imagine releasing any tension or stress associated with it.

Guided Meditation

Use guided meditation recordings or apps that offer mindfulness practices. These often provide soothing instructions and imagery to help you stay focused and relaxed.

Example: Listen to a guided meditation that directs you to visualize a serene natural setting, allowing your mind to find tranquility.

Mindful Walking

Take a leisurely walk and pay close attention to each step, the sensation of your feet hitting the ground, and the rhythm of your breath. Engage your senses by noticing the sights, sounds, and smells around you.

Example: As you walk, silently observe the sensations in your body and the environment without judgment.

In the journey of healing from heartbreak, it's essential to acknowledge the emotional pain while also nurturing your mental well-being. This chapter has explored various strategies, techniques, and resources to help you navigate this challenging phase. From understanding the mental health implications of heartbreak to practicing mindfulness and utilizing therapeutic worksheets, you have the tools to build resilience, foster self-compassion, and cultivate a positive outlook on your healing process. Remember that healing is a gradual process, and with dedication and support, you can emerge stronger, wiser, and ready to embrace new beginnings. As you continue forward, stay open to growth, self-discovery, and the possibility of finding happiness once again.

CHAPTER 5:
PRIORITIZING YOUR EMOTIONAL HEALTH

In the intricate tapestry of human experience, emotions weave a vibrant thread that shapes how we perceive, engage with, and respond to the world around us. This chapter is a guide dedicated to the intricate realm of emotional health—a journey of acknowledging, understanding, and nurturing the wide spectrum of feelings that color our lives. While emotions can be both exhilarating and challenging, they play a pivotal role in our overall well-being. This chapter aims to provide you with insights, tools, and practices to validate your emotions, navigate through them with resilience, and cultivate emotional well-being that empowers you to lead a more fulfilling life. Whether you're seeking to manage stress, process grief, or enhance your emotional intelligence, this chapter will be your companion on the path to fostering a harmonious relationship with your emotional landscape.

Your Emotions Are Valid

Often, we find ourselves navigating through a vast spectrum of feelings, each with its unique hues and shades. It's essential to recognize that every emotion you experience is valid and authentic. Your emotions are not mere fleeting reactions but rather genuine expressions of your inner self.

Society might sometimes impose expectations or judgments on certain emotions, causing you to doubt or suppress what you feel. However, it's crucial to remember that your emotions are your own, arising from your individual experiences, perceptions, and responses. They provide you with valuable insights into your needs, desires, and boundaries.

Embracing the validity of your emotions involves acknowledging that they have a purpose, even if they're challenging or uncomfortable. Each emotion serves as a signal, offering you information about your internal landscape and the world around you. By honoring your feelings, you empower yourself to navigate life with greater authenticity and self-awareness.

Remember that validating your emotions is the first step toward building a more resilient and authentic relationship with yourself. By honoring the full spectrum of your feelings, you set the stage for cultivating emotional well-being and enhancing your overall quality of life.

Healthy Coping Strategies

In the intricate journey of life, we often encounter moments that challenge our emotional resilience and well-being. During these times, practicing healthy coping strategies can be immensely beneficial. These strategies provide constructive ways to navigate difficulties, manage stress, and foster emotional balance.

Building Healthy Habits and Routines

Creating and maintaining healthy habits and routines is an essential aspect of nurturing your emotional well-being and overall quality of life.

By intentionally incorporating positive practices into your daily life, you can cultivate resilience, reduce stress, and enhance your emotional health.

Set Clear Intentions

Begin by identifying the specific habits or routines you want to establish. Whether it's practicing gratitude, engaging in physical activity, or dedicating time to self-care, clear intentions serve as the foundation for building new habits.

Start Small

Begin with manageable steps to avoid feeling overwhelmed. Starting small allows you to gradually integrate new behaviors into your routine without feeling pressured or discouraged.

Consistency is Key

Consistency is vital when building habits. Consistently engaging in a behavior helps solidify it as a routine. Consider setting specific times each day to practice your chosen habit, which will make it easier to stick to.

Create Triggers

Associate your new habit with an existing routine or trigger. For example, if you want to incorporate mindfulness meditation, do it right after brushing your teeth in the morning or before bedtime.

Track Your Progress

Monitoring your progress can provide motivation and a sense of accomplishment. Use a journal, app, or calendar to track your daily efforts and celebrate your achievements.

Be Patient

Building habits takes time and patience. Don't be discouraged by occasional setbacks or missed days. The key is to maintain a positive attitude and resume your efforts.

Accountability

Share your intentions with a friend, family member, or accountability partner. Having someone to check in with can help you stay motivated and committed.

Reward Yourself

Celebrate your successes along the way. Rewarding yourself for sticking to your habit can reinforce positive behavior and make the process more enjoyable.

Flexibility

Life can be unpredictable, so be flexible with yourself. If circumstances prevent you from engaging in your habit at a specific time, find alternative ways to incorporate it into your day.

Reflect and Adjust

Periodically review your habits and routines. Are they contributing positively to your emotional health? If needed, make adjustments to better align with your goals and well-being.

Practicing Self-Care

Prioritizing self-care is an essential component of maintaining and enhancing your emotional health. Engaging in self-care activities helps you recharge, reduce stress, and foster a positive relationship with yourself. By incorporating self-care practices into your routine, you can create a nurturing environment for your emotional well-being.

- ➤ **Prioritize Rest and Sleep:** Ensuring you get sufficient sleep and rest is foundational to emotional well-being. Establish a consistent sleep schedule and create a relaxing bedtime routine to enhance the quality of your sleep.

- ➤ **Exercise Regularly:** Engaging in physical activity releases endorphins, which contribute to improved mood. Find a form of exercise you enjoy, whether it's going for a walk, practicing yoga, or dancing.

- ➤ **Nourish Your Body:** Eat a balanced diet that includes a variety of nutritious foods. Proper nutrition supports your overall well-being and provides the energy you need to navigate your daily life.

- ➤ **Engage in Creative Activities:** Pursue activities that bring you joy and allow you to express yourself creatively. Whether it's painting, writing, or playing a musical instrument, creativity can be a powerful outlet for emotions.

- ➤ **Connect with Others:** Spend time with supportive friends, family members, or social groups. Meaningful connections can provide comfort, understanding, and a sense of belonging.

- ➤ **Unplug:** Disconnect from screens and technology to reduce digital overload. Allocate time to disconnect and engage in activities that don't involve screens.

- ➤ **Pamper Yourself:** Treat yourself to moments of relaxation and indulgence. Whether it's taking a bubble bath, getting a massage, or enjoying a favorite book, pampering can rejuvenate your spirits.

Incorporating self-care practices into your daily routine demonstrates your commitment to nurturing your emotional health. Remember that self-care is a continuous journey, and finding what works best for you may involve trial and error. By prioritizing self-care, you create a foundation of well-being that allows you to navigate life's challenges with greater resilience and a sense of balance.

The Power of Affirmations

Affirmations are powerful tools that can positively influence your emotional well-being and mindset. These positive statements, when repeated regularly, have the potential to shift your thoughts, feelings, and behaviors toward a more optimistic and constructive direction. Incorporating affirmations into your daily routine can be an effective way to boost your self-esteem, build resilience, and foster a positive outlook on life.

How Affirmations Work

Affirmations work by challenging and replacing negative or self-limiting beliefs with positive and empowering thoughts. By repeatedly affirming these positive statements, you create new neural pathways in your brain that reinforce the desired mindset. This process can help you break free from negative thought patterns and cultivate a more supportive inner dialogue.

Using Affirmations for Emotional Well-Being

Here are some steps to effectively incorporate affirmations into your daily routine:

> ➤ **Choose Positive Statements:** Select affirmations that resonate with you and address areas of your emotional well-being that you want to enhance. These statements should be present tense, positive, and specific.

➤ **Be Consistent:** Set aside dedicated time each day to practice affirmations. Consistency is key to reaping the benefits of this practice.

➤ **Repeat Aloud or Write:** Repeat your chosen affirmations aloud or write them down. Speaking them out loud adds a vocal element to the practice while writing them reinforces the message.

➤ **Believe in What You Say:** As you repeat your affirmations, connect with the words and believe in their truth. This emotional connection enhances their effectiveness.

➤ **Visualize:** As you affirm, visualize the positive outcomes associated with the statements. This adds a vivid sensory component to the practice.

Example Affirmations for Emotional Well-Being

➤ I am worthy of love and happiness.

➤ I am resilient and capable of overcoming challenges.

➤ I embrace change and find growth opportunities.

➤ I deserve self-care and compassion.

➤ I release what no longer serves me and make room for positivity.

➤ I am in control of my thoughts and emotions.

➤ I choose peace and positivity in every situation.

➤ I am grateful for the lessons that life presents to me.

➤ I trust in my ability to handle whatever comes my way.

➤ I am enough, just as I am.

By integrating some of these positive affirmations into your daily routine, you can gradually shift your mindset towards one that is more supportive and affirming. Remember that affirmations are a tool that requires practice and patience. Over time, their impact can be profound, contributing to greater emotional well-being, self-confidence, and a more positive outlook on life.

Journaling and Its Benefits

Journaling is a therapeutic practice that offers numerous benefits for prioritizing your emotional health. It provides a safe and private space to express your thoughts, feelings, and experiences, helping you gain insights into your emotions and aiding in the healing process. Here are some of the key advantages of incorporating journaling into your emotional wellness routine:

- ➢ **Emotional Release:** Journaling allows you to release pent-up emotions and thoughts, providing an outlet for feelings that may otherwise remain unexpressed.

- ➢ **Self-Reflection:** Through journaling, you can engage in self-reflection, gaining a deeper understanding of your emotions, triggers, and thought patterns.

- ➢ **Stress Reduction:** Writing about your feelings and experiences can help reduce stress and anxiety by creating a sense of clarity and organization in your mind.

- ➢ **Problem Solving:** Journaling provides an opportunity to work through challenges and find solutions by examining them from different perspectives.

➢ **Increased Self-Awareness:** Regular journaling helps you become more attuned to your emotions and inner world, fostering self-awareness and personal growth.

➢ **Healing and Recovery:** Documenting your thoughts and experiences can aid in the healing process after a breakup or emotional distress, allowing you to track your progress over time.

Journaling Prompts

To make the most of your journaling practice, consider using prompts that encourage deep self-exploration and emotional processing. Here are some example prompts that can guide your journaling journey toward emotional healing:

➢ Describe a recent experience that triggered strong emotions. How did you react, and what did you learn about yourself from this situation?

➢ Reflect on a past relationship that has had a significant impact on your emotional well-being. How has this experience shaped your current feelings and perspectives?

➢ What are some positive qualities or strengths that you possess? How can you use these qualities to support your healing process?

➢ Write a letter to your younger self, offering the compassion and guidance you wish you had received during challenging times.

➢ What are your greatest fears or worries related to healing and moving forward? How can you challenge or reframe these fears?

➢ List three things you're grateful for today. How do these moments of gratitude contribute to your emotional well-being?

➢ Describe an activity or hobby that brings you joy and helps you relax. How can you incorporate more of these activities into your daily life?

➢ Reflect on a setback or obstacle you've faced recently. How can you use this experience as an opportunity for growth and learning?

➢ What are some self-care practices that nourish your emotional health? How can you prioritize these practices in your routine?

➢ Imagine a future version of yourself who has healed and found happiness. What steps can you take to move closer to this vision?

By consistently engaging with these journaling prompts, you can tap into the therapeutic benefits of self-expression, gain clarity about your emotions, and embark on a journey of emotional healing and self-discovery.

Building Your Emotional Support Team

Navigating emotional challenges, especially after a breakup or during difficult times, can be a lot easier when you have a strong support system in place. Building a network of trusted individuals who provide understanding, empathy, and encouragement can significantly contribute to your emotional well-being. Here's how to construct and nurture your emotional support team:

➢ **Identify Potential Supporters:** Begin by identifying individuals in your life who genuinely care about your well-being and whom you feel comfortable opening up to. Friends, family members, colleagues, mentors, or even support groups can all be part of your support network.

➢ **Diverse Sources of Support:** Consider the different types of support you might need. Emotional support, practical advice, and companionship are just a few examples. Diversifying your sources of support can help ensure you receive a well-rounded network of care.

➢ **Communicate Your Needs:** Reach out to potential supporters and express your feelings and needs openly. Let them know how they can best support you, whether it's through active listening, spending time together, or offering advice.

➢ **Set Realistic Expectations:** Understand that not everyone in your life will have the capacity to provide the same level of support. Some individuals might be better at offering emotional support, while others excel at practical assistance.

➢ **Nurture Reciprocal Relationships:** Building a support system is a two-way street. Be prepared to offer your support and be there for your friends and loved ones when they need you. Reciprocity enhances the strength of your emotional connections.

➢ **Establish Boundaries:** While it's important to lean on your support system, it's also essential to maintain your boundaries. Be mindful of not overwhelming any one individual with all your emotional needs.

➤ **Seek Professional Help:** In some cases, seeking support from mental health professionals, such as therapists or counselors, can provide specialized guidance and coping strategies for your unique situation.

➤ **Utilize Technology:** Online communities, forums, and therapy apps can also serve as valuable sources of support, connecting you with individuals who are going through similar experiences.

➤ **Regular Check-Ins:** Keep in touch with your support network regularly, even when you're feeling well. This helps nurture your connections and makes it easier to reach out when you're facing challenges.

Remember that your emotional support team is not fixed—it can evolve over time. As you grow and change, so might your needs and the people who can best provide the support you require. Building and maintaining a strong emotional support network can be a lifeline during times of distress and a source of joy and connection during times of happiness.

Emotional Self-Care Worksheets

Engaging in emotional self-care is essential for maintaining your well-being and nurturing a positive relationship with yourself. These worksheets are designed to guide you through the process of exploring your emotions, practicing self-compassion, and developing strategies for enhancing your emotional health. Here are a few examples of emotional self-care worksheets that you can use:

Identifying Emotions

Instructions: Take a few moments to reflect on your current emotions and fill in the following sections:

Emotion: (Write down the emotion you are experiencing, e.g., "Sadness," "Anxiety," "Happiness.")

_____

Why am I feeling this way? (Briefly describe the situation or trigger that is causing this emotion.)

_____

_____

_____

Intensity: (Rate the intensity of this emotion on a scale of 1 to 10, with 1 being very mild and 10 being extremely intense.)

_____

Physical Sensations: (Note any physical sensations or bodily reactions that accompany this emotion, e.g., "tight chest," "butterflies in the stomach.")

_____

_____

_____

Thoughts: (Write down any thoughts or beliefs that are related to this emotion.)

_____

_____

_____

Duration: (Estimate how long you have been feeling this way.)

_____

_____

_____

Response: (Describe any actions or behaviors that this emotion has led you to engage in.)

_____

_____

_____

Impact: (Reflect on how this emotion is impacting your overall well-being.)

_____

_____

_____

Alternative Perspectives: (Consider alternative ways of interpreting the situation that might lead to a different emotional response.)

_____

_____

_____

Self-Care Action: (List one self-care action you can take to support yourself in managing this emotion.)

_____

_____

_____

Remember, this worksheet is designed to help you become more aware of your emotions and their underlying causes. By completing this exercise, you are taking a step towards understanding and managing your feelings more healthily.

Self-Compassion Journaling Worksheet

Instructions: Take a moment to reflect on a challenging situation you have recently experienced. Use the prompts below to practice self-compassion and understanding towards yourself.

Challenging Situation: (Describe the situation that has been challenging for you.)

_____

_____

_____

Emotional Response: (Write down the emotions you felt in response to this situation.)

_____

_____

_____

Self-Compassion Prompts:

Self-Kindness: Imagine a close friend going through a similar situation. What would you say to them to offer comfort and support? Write down those same kind and supportive words for yourself.

_____

_____

_____

_____

Common Humanity: Remember that everyone faces challenges and difficult emotions at times. Reflect on the shared human experience of suffering. Write down a compassionate reminder that you are not alone in feeling this way.

_____

_____

_____

_____

Mindfulness: Bring awareness to your emotions without judgment. Acknowledge your feelings with an open heart. Write down a statement that acknowledges your emotions without criticizing yourself.

_____

_____

_____

_____

Understanding: Reflect on the factors that might have contributed to your reaction in this situation. Write down an understanding and non-judgmental explanation for why you felt the way you did.

_____

_____

_____

_____

Self-Care Action: List one self-care action you can take to support yourself in this moment of difficulty. This could be something soothing or comforting that helps you feel cared for.

_____

_____

_____

_____

Affirmation: Write down a positive affirmation or statement of self-compassion that you can repeat to yourself whenever you're faced with challenging emotions.

_____

_____

_____

_____

Reflection: Take a moment to reread what you've written and notice how practicing self-compassion has affected your perspective on the challenging situation and your emotions. Remember that self-compassion is an ongoing practice that you can cultivate to support your emotional well-being.

Creating an Emotional Toolkit Worksheet

Instructions: Take some time to create a personalized emotional toolkit filled with strategies and activities that you can turn to when you're feeling down. Think about activities that bring you comfort, joy, relaxation, and a sense of accomplishment. Write down your chosen strategies below.

Comforting Activities:

Activity: (Describe an activity that provides you comfort.)

How It Helps: (Explain how this activity brings you comfort.)

Activity: (Describe an activity that provides you comfort.)

How It Helps: (Explain how this activity brings you comfort.)

___

Joyful Activities:

Activity: (Describe an activity that brings you joy.)

___

How It Makes You Feel: (Describe the positive emotions this activity evokes.)

___

Activity: (Describe an activity that brings you joy.)

___

How It Makes You Feel: (Describe the positive emotions this activity evokes.)

___

Relaxation Strategies:

Strategy: (Describe a relaxation technique you find helpful.)

___

How It Helps: (Explain how this strategy helps you relax.)

___

Strategy: (Describe a relaxation technique you find helpful.)

___

How It Helps: (Explain how this strategy helps you relax.)

___

Sense of Accomplishment Activities:

Activity: (Describe an activity that gives you a sense of accomplishment.)

Why It Matters: (Explain why this activity makes you feel accomplished.)

Activity: (Describe an activity that gives you a sense of accomplishment.)

Why It Matters: (Explain why this activity makes you feel accomplished.)

Using Your Toolkit: When you're feeling down, overwhelmed, or in need of emotional support, turn to your emotional toolkit. Choose one or more activities, strategies, or techniques from the list above that resonate with you in that moment. Remember, your emotional toolkit is a resource you can rely on to nurture your well-being and navigate challenging emotions.

Affirmation Reflection Worksheet

Instructions: Use this worksheet to create and reflect on affirmations that promote positive self-talk and boost self-esteem. Affirmations are statements that reflect qualities and beliefs you want to cultivate within yourself.

Affirmation 1: "I am..."

Why this affirmation resonates with me: (Explain why this affirmation feels meaningful or relevant to you.)

_____

_____

How I can incorporate this affirmation into my daily life: (Describe how you can remind yourself of this affirmation and integrate it into your thoughts.)

_____

_____

_____

Affirmation 2: "I choose..."

_____

Why this affirmation resonates with me: (Explain why this affirmation feels meaningful or relevant to you.)

_____

_____

How I can incorporate this affirmation into my daily life: (Describe how you can remind yourself of this affirmation and integrate it into your thoughts.)

_____

_____

_____

Affirmation 3: "I deserve..."

_____

Why this affirmation resonates with me: (Explain why this affirmation feels meaningful or relevant to you.)

_____

_____

How I can incorporate this affirmation into my daily life: (Describe how you can remind yourself of this affirmation and integrate it into your thoughts.)

_____

_____

Affirmation 4: "I am capable of..."

_____

Why this affirmation resonates with me: (Explain why this affirmation feels meaningful or relevant to you.)

_____

_____

How I can incorporate this affirmation into my daily life: (Describe how you can remind yourself of this affirmation and integrate it into your thoughts.)

_____

_____

_____

Affirmation 5: "I embrace..."

_____

Why this affirmation resonates with me: (Explain why this affirmation feels meaningful or relevant to you.)

_____

_____

How I can incorporate this affirmation into my daily life: (Describe how you can remind yourself of this affirmation and integrate it into your thoughts.)

_____

_____

_____

Reflection: Take a moment to reflect on the affirmations you've written. How do these affirmations contribute to your overall self-esteem and well-being? How can you use them to foster a positive and confident mindset? Remember that affirmations are tools you can use to uplift yourself and shape your thoughts in a more empowering direction.

_____

_____

_____

_____

Building Emotional Resilience Worksheet

Instructions: Use this worksheet to build emotional resilience by reflecting on past challenging experiences and how you've coped with them. By identifying your strengths and coping strategies, you can empower yourself to face future challenges with confidence.

Step 1: Recall a Challenging Experience

Think of a challenging experience you've faced in the past. It could be a difficult breakup, a career setback, or a personal struggle. Write down a brief description of the situation.

Challenging Experience:

_____

_____

_____

Step 2: Your Emotional Response

Describe how you felt during this challenging experience. What were the emotions that arose? Be honest about the feelings you experienced.

Emotional Response:

_____

_____

Step 3: Coping Strategies

List the strategies or actions you took to cope with this challenging experience. These could be things you did to manage your emotions, seek support, or problem-solve.

Coping Strategies:

_____

_____

_____

Step 4: Strengths

Identify the strengths or qualities you demonstrated during this difficult time. What personal attributes or skills did you rely on to navigate the situation?

Strengths:

_____

_____

_____

Step 5: Reflection

Reflect on how you've grown or learned from this challenging experience. What insights or lessons have you gained that contribute to your emotional resilience?

Reflection:

_____

_____

_____

_____

Step 6: Applying Resilience

Think about how you can apply the coping strategies and strengths you've identified to future challenges. How can these experiences guide you in building emotional resilience for what lies ahead?

Applying Resilience:

_____

_____

_____

Building emotional resilience involves acknowledging your ability to overcome challenges and learn from them. By recognizing your strengths and developing effective coping strategies, you can approach life's difficulties with greater confidence and adaptability.

Gratitude and Positive Reflection Worksheet

Instructions: Use this worksheet to cultivate gratitude and a positive outlook by focusing on the positive aspects of your life. Reflect on things you're grateful for, positive moments, and achievements that contribute to an optimistic perspective.

Step 1: Gratitude List

Write down three things you're grateful for in your life. These could be people, experiences, or things that bring you joy and appreciation.

_____

_____

_____

Step 2: Positive Moments

Recall a recent positive moment that made you feel happy or content. Describe the experience and how it made you feel.

Positive Moment:

_____

_____

_____

Step 3: Personal Achievements

Think about an achievement you're proud of, no matter how small. It could be related to work, personal growth, or relationships. Write down the achievement and why it's meaningful to you.

Achievement:

_____

_____

_____

Step 4: Reflection

Reflect on how focusing on gratitude and positive aspects of your life impacts your overall outlook. How does recognizing the good things in your life contribute to your emotional well-being?

Reflection:

_____

_____

_____

_____

Step 5: Future Focus

Consider how you can continue to cultivate gratitude and positive reflection in your daily life. Are there specific practices or habits you can adopt to maintain an optimistic perspective?

Future Focus:

_____

_____

_____

_____

Practicing gratitude and positive reflection is a powerful way to shift your focus from challenges to the positive aspects of your life. By acknowledging the good moments, achievements, and things you're grateful for, you can foster a more optimistic and joyful mindset.

Emotional Self-Care Plan Worksheet

Instructions: Use this worksheet to create a personalized emotional self-care plan that supports your emotional well-being. List self-care activities, their frequency, and the positive impact they have on your emotions.

Step 1: Self-Care Activities

List self-care activities that help you relax, recharge, and manage your emotions. These can be simple activities you enjoy.

1. _____

2. _____

3. _____

Step 2: Frequency

Indicate how often you plan to engage in each self-care activity. This could be daily, weekly, or as needed.

1. Activity: _____

   Frequency: _____

2. Activity: _____

   Frequency: _____

3. Activity: _____

   Frequency: _____

4. Activity: _____

   Frequency: _____

5. Activity: _____

   Frequency: _____

Step 3: Positive Impact

Write down how each self-care activity positively impacts your emotional well-being. Consider how it makes you feel and why it's important for your self-care.

1. Activity: _____

   Frequency: _____

2. Activity: _____

   Frequency: _____

3. Activity: _____

   Frequency: _____

4. Activity: _____

   Frequency: _____

5. Activity: _____

   Frequency: _____

Step 4: Commitment

Reflect on your commitment to prioritize your emotional self-care. How important is it for you to engage in these activities regularly to support your emotional well-being?

Commitment:

Step 5: Integration

Think about how you can integrate these self-care activities into your routine. Are there specific times of day or situations when you can engage in them?

Integration:

Creating an emotional self-care plan is a proactive way to prioritize your emotional well-being. By engaging in self-care activities and recognizing their positive impact, you're taking steps to maintain a healthy and balanced emotional state. Using these worksheets can facilitate your journey toward emotional well-being. They provide structure and guidance for exploring your emotions, practicing self-compassion, and developing healthy habits to nurture your emotional health. Remember that emotional self-care is a personal journey, and these worksheets are tools to support you along the way.

PART 3:

A BETTER YOU

In this section, we will delve into the journey of self-discovery and growth after a breakup. Part 3, A Better You, focuses on reclaiming your sense of self, finding closure from the past, and fostering healthy relationships. These chapters will guide you through the process of rebuilding your identity, moving forward with a renewed perspective, and developing the skills to build and maintain positive connections. As you walk this path of personal transformation, you'll gain insights into nurturing your well-being and creating a brighter future.

CHAPTER 6:
REBUILDING YOUR IDENTITY

In the aftermath of a breakup, the task of rediscovering your identity can feel both liberating and daunting. Rebuilding your identity, the focus of this chapter is vital as you "find" yourself again as an individual rather than part of a couple. As you navigate the intricacies of separation, this chapter offers insights into how you can reclaim your sense of self, foster your independence, and cultivate newfound confidence. By understanding the steps to reconnecting with who you are at your core, you can pave the way for a stronger, more authentic version of yourself.

When Your Self-Esteem Has Taken a Huge Blow

A breakup can often leave a lasting impact on your self-esteem, shaking the foundation of how you perceive yourself. The emotional turmoil, feelings of rejection, and self-doubt that can accompany a breakup might lead you to question your worth, capabilities, attractiveness, and overall value. This section delves into this critical aspect of healing by offering insights and strategies to navigate the challenges of rebuilding your self-esteem.

Recognizing Signs of Low Self-Esteem

It's important to be aware of the signs that indicate your self-esteem might be compromised. Some common signs include pervasive negative self-talk, a tendency to compare yourself unfavorably to others, a constant fear of judgment or rejection, and difficulty asserting yourself in various situations. Understanding these signs can be the first step towards addressing and rebuilding your self-esteem.

Strategies to Raise Your Self-Esteem

This section provides practical strategies to help you raise your self-esteem and nurture a positive self-image. These strategies encompass self-compassion, practicing self-care, setting realistic goals, celebrating achievements, focusing on your strengths, and challenging negative thought patterns. By engaging in these practices consistently, you can gradually shift your self-perception from one of self-doubt to one of self-acceptance and confidence.

Cultivating a Healthy Self-Image

Rebuilding your self-esteem after a breakup is a journey of self-discovery and self-acceptance. It involves recognizing your inherent worth, embracing your unique qualities, and acknowledging that your value is not determined solely by external factors. Try to remember that self-esteem is not about perfection but about self-compassion, resilience, and growth.

Embracing a Positive Mindset

Cultivating a positive mindset is crucial in your efforts to rebuild your self-esteem. Surround yourself with supportive people who uplift you, engage in activities that make you feel accomplished, and practice gratitude to shift your focus towards the positive aspects of your life. By fostering a mindset that values and nurtures your self-worth, you can gradually overcome the impact of a breakup on your self-esteem.

Self-Esteem Boosters

Rebuilding your self-esteem after a breakup requires intentional effort and a commitment to nurturing a positive self-image. This section is designed to provide you with a collection of effective strategies and techniques to elevate your self-esteem and foster a healthier sense of self-worth. These self-esteem boosters can empower you to regain confidence, embrace your strengths, and cultivate a more resilient mindset.

Practice Self-Compassion

Self-compassion is the foundation of healthy self-esteem. Treat yourself with the same kindness, understanding, and patience that you would offer a friend. Acknowledge your imperfections without judgment and practice self-forgiveness. By cultivating self-compassion, you create an environment of acceptance that supports your journey towards higher self-esteem.

Surround Yourself with Positivity

Choose to surround yourself with people who uplift and support you. Distance yourself from individuals who undermine your self-esteem or foster negativity. Positive relationships can contribute to a more positive self-concept and a greater sense of belonging.

Celebrate Your Strengths

Identify your strengths and unique qualities. Reflect on your achievements, skills, and attributes that make you special. By recognizing and celebrating these aspects of yourself, you can enhance your self-esteem and reinforce a sense of value.

Accept Imperfection

Nobody is perfect, and embracing your imperfections is essential for building healthy self-esteem. Accept that making mistakes is a natural part of life and an opportunity for growth. Instead of dwelling on shortcomings, focus on learning and improving.

Seek Professional Support

If rebuilding your self-esteem feels overwhelming, consider seeking the guidance of a therapist or counselor. Professional support can offer tailored strategies and insights to address the specific challenges you're facing and provide a safe space to explore your feelings and beliefs.

Building Self-Confidence

Self-confidence is a key pillar of a strong and resilient identity. It empowers you to embrace challenges, take risks, and navigate life with a sense of assurance. This section provides you with a comprehensive toolkit of strategies and techniques to cultivate and enhance your self-confidence. By incorporating these practices into your life, you can embark on a journey of self-discovery and personal growth that leads to greater self-assurance.

Acknowledge Your Achievements

Reflect on your past achievements, both big and small. Recognize the challenges you've overcome, the goals you've achieved, and the progress you've made. By acknowledging your successes, you reinforce your ability to succeed in future endeavors.

Step Out of Your Comfort Zone

Embrace opportunities that push you outside your comfort zone. Facing new challenges and experiences not only expands your skill set but also proves to yourself that you're capable of adapting and thriving in different situations.

Celebrate Your Unique Qualities

Recognize and embrace your unique qualities, strengths, and talents. Each person has something special to offer, and acknowledging your individuality fosters a sense of pride and self-confidence.

Visualize Success

Engage in visualization exercises where you imagine yourself succeeding in various scenarios. Visualization can help boost your confidence by allowing you to mentally practice success and build a positive association with achieving your goals.

Seek Feedback

Request feedback from trusted friends, family members, or mentors. Constructive feedback can provide valuable insights into your strengths and areas for growth, helping you improve and build confidence.

Learn and Adapt

View challenges and setbacks as opportunities to learn and grow. Embracing a growth mindset allows you to see failure as a stepping stone toward success rather than a reflection of your worth.

Seek Personal Development

Engage in continuous personal development through learning, skill-building, and self-discovery. Gaining new knowledge and honing your skills can boost your sense of competence and self-assurance.

Re-Establishing Your Independence

After experiencing a breakup, it's essential to rediscover your sense of independence and autonomy. Reclaiming your individuality empowers you to make decisions that align with your values and aspirations. This section provides insights and strategies to help you regain your self-sufficiency and build a life that's fulfilling on your terms.

Rediscover Your Passions

Reflect on the activities and hobbies that once brought you joy. Reconnecting with your interests and passions can reignite your sense of purpose and provide a meaningful outlet for self-expression.

Set Personal Boundaries

Establish clear boundaries in your relationships, both with friends and family. Communicate your needs and limits, ensuring that you prioritize your well-being and emotional health.

Practice Decision-Making

Make decisions that reflect your desires and aspirations. Rebuilding your independence involves taking ownership of your choices and steering your life in directions that resonate with you.

Embrace Solo Adventures

Engage in solo adventures and experiences. Whether it's traveling to a new destination, dining at a favorite restaurant, or attending events, embracing solo activities can boost your confidence and sense of autonomy.

Build a Support System

While independence is important, having a supportive network is equally vital. Surround yourself with friends, family, and mentors who uplift and encourage you as you navigate your journey.

Focus on Personal Growth

Set goals for personal growth and development. Pursue education, skill-building, and self-improvement endeavors that align with your interests and aspirations.

Develop Financial Literacy

Take charge of your financial well-being by enhancing your financial literacy. Understanding your finances empowers you to make informed decisions that support your independence.

Explore New Social Circles

Expand your social circle by meeting new people and participating in social activities. Broadening your connections can introduce fresh perspectives and opportunities for growth.

Self-Reflection is Important

Amid the process of rebuilding after a breakup, self-reflection emerges as a crucial tool for self-discovery and growth. Taking the time to introspect and understand your feelings, thoughts, and experiences allows you to navigate your journey of healing and transformation. This section emphasizes the importance of self-reflection and provides valuable insights into how it can aid your emotional recovery and personal development.

Gain Clarity on Your Emotions

Delve into your emotions and thoughts surrounding the breakup. Reflect on the range of feelings you're experiencing and explore the reasons behind them. By gaining clarity on your emotions, you can better understand your needs and take steps toward healing.

Identify Lessons Learned

Breakups often come with valuable lessons. Reflect on what you've learned from the relationship, the breakup itself, and your subsequent experiences. Identifying these lessons helps you grow and make more informed choices in the future.

Reevaluate Your Goals

During this time of change, it's opportune to reassess your life goals and priorities. Reflect on your personal and professional aspirations, considering how they align with your evolving sense of self.

Discover Personal Strengths

Reflect on your strengths and qualities that have helped you get through previous challenges. Recognizing these attributes boosts your self-esteem and empowers you to face adversity with confidence.

Understand Patterns and Triggers

Self-reflection aids in recognizing patterns and triggers in your past relationships. By identifying recurring themes, you can work to break negative cycles and make healthier choices moving forward.

Clarify Your Values

Reflect on your core values and beliefs. Are they aligned with the relationships you've pursued? Evaluating your values can guide your decisions and help you seek connections that resonate with your authentic self.

Set Boundaries for the Future

Based on your reflections, establish clear boundaries for future relationships. Identifying what you're comfortable with and what you're not helps you prioritize your well-being and emotional health.

Practice Self-Compassion

As you reflect, remember to treat yourself with kindness and compassion. Acknowledge any self-criticism that arises and work to reframe it with self-compassionate thoughts.

Develop a Personal Growth Plan

Use your reflections to develop a plan for personal growth and self-improvement. Set achievable goals that align with your insights and aim to nurture your emotional well-being.

Enhance Self-Awareness

Engaging in self-reflection enhances your self-awareness, allowing you to tune into your thoughts, feelings, and behaviors. This awareness lays the foundation for making conscious choices that align with your true self.

Cultivate Resilience

By reflecting on the challenges you've faced and overcome, you can cultivate emotional resilience. Recognize your ability to adapt and thrive even in the face of adversity.

Prioritize Healing

Self-reflection supports your healing journey by helping you make sense of your experiences and emotions. It allows you to create a roadmap for recovery that acknowledges your feelings and empowers you to move forward.

Self Esteem Worksheets

Self-esteem plays a pivotal role in our overall well-being and how we perceive ourselves. Building and nurturing healthy self-esteem is essential for emotional resilience and personal growth. This section introduces a series of self-esteem worksheets designed to guide you through the journey of self-discovery, self-acceptance, and self-improvement. These worksheets provide you with practical exercises to enhance your self-esteem, boost your self-confidence, and foster a positive self-image.

Identifying Self-Defeating Thoughts

This worksheet is designed to help you become aware of negative and self-defeating thoughts that may be impacting your self-esteem. By identifying these thoughts, you can work towards replacing them with healthier and more positive alternatives. Follow the steps below to complete the worksheet:

Step 1: Self-Defeating Thought Identification

Write down any negative thoughts or self-critical statements that come to mind. These might be thoughts that contribute to feelings of low self-esteem, self-doubt, or inadequacy.

Step 2: Challenge and Reframe

Next, challenge these negative thoughts by asking yourself if they are based on evidence or if they are simply assumptions. Reframe each thought into a more balanced and positive statement.

Step 3: Affirmations

Create positive affirmations based on the reframed thoughts. These affirmations will serve as positive self-talk to counteract self-defeating thoughts.

Step 4: Practice

Make an effort to replace self-defeating thoughts with the positive affirmations you've created. Practice this exercise regularly to reinforce positive self-talk and boost your self-esteem.

Remember, the goal is not to eliminate all negative thoughts but to become more aware of them and challenge their accuracy. By doing so, you can create a healthier and more compassionate relationship with yourself.

Affirming Your Strengths Worksheet

This worksheet is designed to help you recognize and affirm your strengths, talents, and positive qualities. By acknowledging and listing these attributes as affirmations, you can cultivate a more positive and confident self-perception. Follow the steps below to complete the worksheet.

Step 1: Reflect on Your Strengths

Take a moment to think about your strengths, talents, and positive qualities. Consider your personal achievements, skills, and characteristics that make you unique and capable.

Step 2: Formulate Positive Affirmations

For each strength, talent, or positive quality you've listed, turn it into a positive affirmation. Affirmations are positive statements that help boost your self-confidence and self-belief.

Step 3: Daily Practice

Incorporate these affirmations into your daily routine. Repeat them to yourself in the morning or whenever you need a confidence boost. By consistently affirming your strengths, you can enhance your self-perception and build a stronger sense of self.

Remember, your strengths and positive qualities are an integral part of who you are. Embrace and celebrate them to nurture your self-esteem and overall well-being.

Building a Positive Self-Image Worksheet

This worksheet encourages you to create a visual representation of your positive self-image through creative expression. Engaging in this activity can help reinforce a healthier and more confident self-concept. Follow the steps below to complete the worksheet.

Step 1: Gather Your Materials

Collect materials that will allow you to express yourself creatively. You might need drawing supplies, magazines for collages, colored markers, stickers, or any other items that resonate with you.

Step 2: Reflect on Your Positive Qualities

Take a moment to reflect on your positive qualities, strengths, and attributes that contribute to your self-image. Consider how you want to portray these qualities visually.

Step 3: Create Your Visual Representation

Using the materials you've gathered, start creating your visual representation. This could be in the form of a drawing, collage, or any other creative medium you prefer.

Step 4: Incorporate Affirmations

Integrate positive affirmations into your artwork. These can be statements that align with your desired self-image and reinforce your self-confidence.

Step 5: Embrace Your Creation

Once your visual representation is complete, take a step back and admire your creation. Allow yourself to appreciate the positive qualities and attributes you've highlighted.

Step 6: Display Your Artwork

Place your artwork in a location where you'll frequently see it. This could be in your room, workspace, or any other area that you visit often. Let it serve as a daily reminder of your positive self-image.

Remember, this activity is meant to celebrate your unique qualities and help you view yourself in a more positive light. Let your creative expression guide you toward a more confident and empowered self-concept.

Cultivating Self-Approval Worksheet

This worksheet is designed to help you cultivate self-approval and prioritize your own opinions and beliefs over seeking external validation. Follow the steps below to work through this process.

Step 1: Reflect on External Validation

Take a moment to think about how often you seek external validation from others. Consider situations where you might have valued others' opinions more than your own.

_____

_____

_____

_____

Step 2: Identify Your Values and Opinions

List your core values and beliefs that are important to you. Reflect on why these values matter and how they contribute to your sense of self.

_____

_____

_____

_____

Step 3: Challenge the Need for Approval

Examine situations where you typically seek approval from others. Ask yourself whether their validation truly aligns with your values and opinions.

Step 4: Practice Self-Approval

Think of a recent situation where you sought external validation. Reflect on how you could have approved of yourself and your choices without relying on others' opinions.

Step 5: Affirm Your Self-Worth

Write down affirmations that reinforce your self-worth and emphasize your ability to make valuable decisions based on your beliefs.

Step 6: Embrace Your Authenticity

Remind yourself that seeking self-approval and valuing your opinions is a journey toward authenticity and personal empowerment.

_____

_____

_____

Step 7: Set Intentions

Identify specific areas of your life where you want to prioritize self-approval over external validation. Set intentions to practice this mindset shift in those situations.

_____

_____

_____

These self-esteem worksheets provide valuable tools for enhancing your self-image, boosting your confidence, and fostering a greater sense of self-worth. Engaging with these exercises empowers you to actively shape your self-perception and embark on a journey of improved emotional well-being and self-acceptance.

Worksheets for Self-Rediscovery

The journey of self-rediscovery is a transformative process that involves exploring your inner thoughts, feelings, and beliefs to gain a deeper understanding of yourself. These worksheets are designed to guide you through introspective exercises that facilitate self-awareness, self-acceptance, and personal growth. Engaging with these worksheets can help you reconnect with your true essence and uncover valuable insights about your identity, values, and aspirations.

Exploring Your Personal Identity Worksheet

Use this worksheet to delve into different facets of your identity and gain a deeper understanding of who you are. Reflect on the following areas to align your life with your authentic self:

Roles: List the roles you currently hold in your life, such as parent, friend, employee, etc. Reflect on how each role contributes to your sense of identity and fulfillment.

_____

_____

Strengths: Identify the strengths and qualities that you value most about yourself. Consider both your innate strengths and those you've developed over time.

_____

_____

Values: List your core values—the principles that guide your decisions and actions. Reflect on how your values influence your choices and contribute to your identity.

_____

_____

Passions: Explore your passions and interests that bring you joy and excitement. Consider how these activities contribute to your sense of self.

_____

_____

Beliefs: Reflect on your beliefs about yourself, others, and the world. Examine how these beliefs shape your identity and the way you interact with the world.

_____

_____

Goals: Think about your short-term and long-term goals. Consider how these goals reflect your desires and aspirations, contributing to your sense of identity.

_____

_____

Interests: List hobbies, activities, or subjects you enjoy exploring in your free time. Reflect on how these interests add richness to your identity.

_____

_____

Accomplishments: Write down significant accomplishments you're proud of. Reflect on how these achievements contribute to your sense of self-worth.

_____

_____

Relationships: Consider your relationships with family, friends, and loved ones. Reflect on how these connections shape your identity and support your growth.

_____

_____

Self-Image: Reflect on your self-image and how you perceive yourself. Consider any areas where you'd like to improve your self-image.

_____

_____

Authenticity: Think about how well your current lifestyle aligns with your authentic self. Identify areas where you might need to make adjustments.

_____

_____

Action Steps: Based on your reflections, list one or two action steps you can take to align your life more closely with your authentic identity.

_____

_____

Uncovering Your Core Values Worksheet

Use this worksheet to explore and uncover your core values, which are the guiding principles that shape your life's decisions and actions. By identifying your core values, you can live a more authentic and fulfilling life.

Reflection: Take a moment to reflect on your life and the values that have been important to you. Consider experiences, people, and moments that resonate with your sense of what truly matters.

_____

_____

_____

_____

List of Values: Below, you'll find a list of common core values. Review the list and circle the values that resonate with you the most. Feel free to add any values that are not on the list.

➤ Authenticity

➤ Compassion

➤ Creativity

➤ Family

➤ Freedom

➤ Growth

➤ Honesty

➤ Integrity

➤ Joy

➤ Kindness

➤ Learning

➤ Love

➤ Passion

➤ Respect

➤ Responsibility

➤ Success

➤ Trust

➤ Wisdom

_____

_____

_____

Prioritizing Values: From the circled values, choose the top 5 values that feel the most significant to you. These are the values that you want to prioritize in your life.

Reflect on Each Value: For each of your top 5 values, take a moment to reflect on why it's important to you. Consider how this value influences your decisions, relationships, and overall sense of fulfillment.

Aligning with Values: Think about recent decisions or actions you've taken. Do they align with your top values? If not, how might you adjust your choices to better reflect your core values?

Setting Intentions: Write down one or two intentions for how you can live in alignment with each of your top values. Consider specific actions or changes you can make to honor these values.

_____

_____

Review and Reassess: Regularly review your core values and how well your choices align with them. As you grow and evolve, your values may also shift. Be open to reassessing and adjusting your values over time.

_____

_____

Action Steps: List one actionable step you can take for each value to actively incorporate it into your daily life.

_____

_____

Your core values are unique to you, and they play a significant role in shaping your identity and decisions. Use this worksheet as a tool to gain clarity on what truly matters to you and strive to live in alignment with your core values for a more fulfilling life.

Identifying Limiting Beliefs Worksheet

Use this worksheet to identify and challenge limiting beliefs that may be holding you back from reaching your full potential. By recognizing and reframing these beliefs, you can create a more empowering and positive mindset.

Self-Reflection: Take a moment to reflect on areas of your life where you feel stuck or challenged. Consider any thoughts or beliefs that might contribute to these feelings.

_____

_____

List of Beliefs: Below, you'll find a list of common limiting beliefs. Review the list and circle any beliefs that resonate with you or that you've noticed in your thinking.

- ➢ I'm not good enough.
- ➢ I don't deserve success.
- ➢ I'm always unlucky.
- ➢ I can't change.
- ➢ I'm too old/young.
- ➢ Others are better than me.
- ➢ I'm a failure.
- ➢ I'll never succeed.
- ➢ It's too late for me.
- ➢ I'm not smart/talented enough.
- ➢ I'm not attractive enough.
- ➢ I don't have what it takes.
- ➢ I'll be rejected if I try.
- ➢ I can't trust anyone.
- ➢ Life is unfair.

Identifying Your Beliefs: From the circled beliefs, choose the ones that you believe might be limiting you in some way. Write them down.

_____

_____

_____

_____

Challenging Your Beliefs: For each selected belief, ask yourself:

> ➢ Is this belief based on facts or assumptions?

_____

_____

> ➢ What evidence do I have that supports or contradicts this belief?

_____

_____

> ➢ How has this belief held me back in the past?

_____

_____

> ➢ How might my life be different if I didn't hold onto this belief?

_____

_____

Reframing Your Beliefs: For each limiting belief, create a more empowering and positive alternative belief. Focus on statements that encourage growth, self-compassion, and possibility.

_____

_____

_____

_____

Action Steps: Write down one action step you can take to challenge each of your identified limiting beliefs. This could include trying new experiences, seeking support, or practicing self-compassion.

_____

_____

_____

_____

Daily Awareness: Make an effort to be aware of when these limiting beliefs arise in your thoughts. When you catch yourself thinking about them, gently replace them with the positive alternative beliefs you've created.

Review and Progress: Regularly review your progress in challenging and reframing your limiting beliefs. Celebrate your successes and acknowledge the areas where you're still growing.

_____

_____

_____

_____

Engaging with these self-rediscovery worksheets empowers you to embark on a transformative journey of self-discovery and personal growth. Through introspection, reflection, and exploration, you can uncover your authentic self, align with your values, and create a life that resonates with your true essence.

CHAPTER 7:
MOVING ON AND FINDING CLOSURE

In this chapter, we explore the steps involved in moving on and finding closure after experiencing a difficult breakup. The essence of this chapter lies in the powerful message of releasing the grip of the past and embracing the potential of the future. As we delve into the art of letting go, we'll discover how to free ourselves from the chains of past relationships and pave the way for new beginnings. By navigating the path of healing and growth, we can learn to break free from the shackles of heartache and open our hearts to the possibilities that lie ahead. This chapter offers insights, strategies, and exercises to guide you through the process of finding closure and embracing the exciting journey of personal evolution.

Stop Holding On

Letting go is an essential step in the healing process after a breakup. This milestone requires us to untangle the emotional bonds that keep us attached to a relationship that has ended. The act of holding on can prolong our pain and hinder our ability to move forward. In this section, we'll explore effective strategies to help you release your grip on the past and embrace the present and future.

Recognizing the Need for Release

Holding on to a relationship that has come to an end can be fueled by emotions like fear, nostalgia, or a reluctance to face change. It's crucial to recognize when these feelings are causing more harm than good. Acknowledging the need to let go is the first step towards finding closure.

Acceptance as a Path to Healing

Acceptance is a powerful catalyst for healing. Embracing the reality that the relationship is over allows you to reclaim your emotional well-being. This involves acknowledging your emotions and the pain associated with the breakup while also acknowledging that the future holds promise.

Creating Emotional Boundaries

Cutting emotional ties with a past relationship involves creating boundaries that protect your emotional well-being. This means limiting contact with your former partner and removing triggers that remind you of the relationship such as messages on social media. By establishing these boundaries, you can create space for healing and growth.

Engaging in Self-Care

Redirecting your focus from the past to the present is crucial for moving on. Practicing self-care helps you nurture your emotional and physical well-being, fostering a sense of empowerment and autonomy. Engaging in activities that bring you joy, spending time with loved ones, and pursuing your interests can help shift your attention away from holding on.

Why You Need to Move On

Moving on after a breakup is often easier said than done, but it's a critical step towards your emotional well-being and personal growth. Holding on to a relationship that has ended can have detrimental effects on your mental and emotional health. In this section, we'll delve into the reasons why moving on is essential for your healing journey.

Embracing the Present and Future

Holding onto a past relationship can prevent you from fully experiencing the present moment and embracing future opportunities. It's essential to free yourself from the emotional baggage of the past to open the door to new experiences and relationships that align with your growth.

Breaking the Cycle of Pain

Continuously revisiting memories and emotions attached to a past relationship can perpetuate a cycle of pain and prevent you from finding closure. It's important to stop going to places you went to with your ex – at least for a while – and discover new places and build new memories. Letting go allows you to break free from the pain cycle, creating space for healing and transformation.

Rediscovering Yourself

A breakup offers a chance for self-discovery and self-renewal. By moving on, you can redirect your focus toward understanding yourself better, your passions, and your goals. This process allows you to reclaim your identity and build a stronger sense of self. Try new hobbies, and new foods, and visit places you wouldn't have before.

Fostering Emotional Healing

Holding onto a relationship that has ended can keep you stuck in a state of emotional turmoil. Moving on facilitates emotional healing by allowing you to process your feelings, acknowledge your pain, and gradually release it. This process is crucial for achieving a sense of closure and inner peace.

Gaining Perspective

Moving on provides an opportunity to gain perspective on the relationship. As you distance yourself emotionally, you can see the relationship and its dynamics more clearly. This perspective can lead to insights about what you want and need in future relationships.

Empowering Yourself

Choosing to move on is an act of self-empowerment. It's a declaration that you value your emotional well-being and refuse to let the past define your future. By taking this step, you regain control over your life and your happiness.

Embracing Growth and Transformation

Ultimately, moving on from a past relationship is a path to growth and transformation. It signifies your willingness to evolve, learn from your experiences, and create a future that is aligned with your authentic self.

How to Let Go of the Past and Move On

Letting go of the past and finding closure after a breakup is a challenging but necessary step on your journey toward healing and personal growth. Here, we'll explore effective strategies to help you release emotional attachments, gain closure, and move forward with a renewed sense of purpose and well-being.

Allow Yourself to Grieve

Permit yourself to feel the full range of emotions that come with a breakup. Allow yourself to grieve the loss of the relationship and the future you had envisioned.

Create Boundaries

Establish clear boundaries with your ex-partner. This may involve limiting or cutting off contact for a while to give yourself space to heal.

Reflect on the Relationship

Take time to reflect on the relationship and its dynamics. What did you learn? What were the positive and negative aspects? What mistakes did you make and what can you take away from that? This reflection can bring clarity and closure.

Release Resentment and Anger

Holding onto resentment and anger only prolongs the healing process. Practice forgiveness, not for your ex-partner's sake but for your emotional well-being.

Set New Goals

Redirect your focus toward setting new personal and professional goals. Perhaps you'd like to train for a marathon in a year or save up for a trip. Maybe you'd like to aim for that promotion at work or redecorate your office. This shift in focus can help you look forward to the future with excitement and anticipation.

Avoid Idealizing the Past

Remember that it's common to idealize the past after a breakup. Remind yourself of the reasons the relationship ended and the challenges you faced.

Embrace New Experiences

Explore new activities, hobbies, or interests that you've always wanted to pursue. Embracing new experiences can help you create a sense of novelty and adventure in your life.

Rebuild Your Identity

Rediscover yourself and your passions. Use this time to explore new facets of your identity and create a stronger sense of self. You might like to explore a new way of dressing or try a new hairstyle. Watch a different genre of movie than what you normally enjoy or explore music you don't usually listen to.

Focus on Personal Growth

View this period as an opportunity for personal growth and self-improvement. Invest in your education, career, and personal development. There are many free courses online that can enhance your skills and help you build new networks.

Celebrate Progress

Acknowledge and celebrate the progress you make along your healing journey. Small victories can contribute to your overall well-being.

Stay Open to New Possibilities

While it's essential to first let go of the past, remain open to new relationships and experiences. Moving on allows you to create space for positive opportunities.

Setting Goals for the Future

Looking ahead and setting meaningful goals for your future is a powerful way to shift your focus away from the past and into the possibilities that lie ahead. By channeling your energy into positive and purposeful endeavors, you can create a sense of direction and motivation that propels you forward. Here, we'll explore effective strategies for setting goals that align with your personal growth and aspirations.

Reflect on Your Passions and Interests

Take time to reflect on what truly brings you joy and fulfillment. Consider the activities, hobbies, and interests that have always resonated with you. Also, consider the things that you have always wanted to try but haven't yet.

Define Clear and Specific Goals

Create clear and specific goals that are both attainable and challenging. Break down large goals into smaller, actionable steps to make them more manageable. For instance, rather than aiming to repaint your entire apartment, focus on doing one room at a time.

Prioritize Your Well-Being

Set goals that prioritize your physical, emotional, and mental well-being. Whether it's improving your fitness by joining a running group, practicing mindfulness with a yoga class, or seeking therapy, make self-care a cornerstone of your goals. Make a point of planning and shopping for healthy meals for yourself, even if you're eating alone.

Align with Your Values

Ensure that your goals align with your core values and beliefs. When your goals are in harmony with your values, you'll find a deeper sense of purpose and motivation.

Create a Vision Board

Visualize your goals by creating a vision board. Gather images, quotes, and symbols that represent your aspirations and display them where you can see them daily. For instance, maybe you want to book a cruise. Find images of the ship and its destinations for your board.

Set Both Short-Term and Long-Term Goals

Balance your goals between short-term achievements and long-term aspirations. Short-term goals provide a sense of almost instant gratification and accomplishment, while long-term goals give you direction and purpose.

Embrace New Experiences

Challenge yourself to step out of your comfort zone and embrace new experiences. This could involve travel, trying new activities such as a dance or cooking class, or engaging with different communities such as volunteering to help at a soup kitchen.

Break Through Limiting Beliefs

Identify and challenge any limiting beliefs that may be holding you back from setting ambitious goals. Replace negative self-talk with empowering affirmations. For instance, instead of, "I can't even draw a stick man" say, "If I join that drawing class, I will learn how to draw basic pictures."

Celebrate Milestones

Acknowledge and celebrate your achievements along the way. Rewarding yourself for reaching milestones reinforces a positive cycle of progress.

Setting Healthy Boundaries

In addition to setting goals, it's crucial to establish healthy boundaries, especially when dealing with past relationships. Boundaries protect your emotional well-being and ensure that you're prioritizing your needs. Here are some steps to consider:

Reflect on what boundaries are essential to your well-being. Consider aspects such as communication, social interactions, and personal space.

You might want to change the route you drive to work, change your phone number, or remove yourself from social media for a while. You may want to consider changing the locks on your home.

Articulate your boundaries with your ex-partner, friends, and family. Effective communication helps prevent misunderstandings and ensures that your needs are respected. For example, asking people not to call you after 8 p.m.

If necessary, create physical and emotional distance from your ex-partner to give yourself space to heal and move on. Consider limiting or unfollowing your ex-partner on social media to prevent unnecessary emotional triggers. A more drastic measure is to move homes. Is there somewhere else you've always wanted to live and work?

Setting goals and establishing healthy boundaries are essential steps in moving on from the past and creating a brighter future. By focusing on your personal growth, well-being, and aspirations, you'll empower yourself to build a life that is aligned with your authentic self and values.

Embracing New Opportunities and Experiences

Moving on from a past relationship provides a unique opportunity to embrace new possibilities and experiences. While the end of a relationship may initially feel like a loss, reframing it as a chance for growth and self-discovery can open doors to exciting opportunities. By stepping outside your comfort zone and exploring new horizons, you can create a more fulfilling and enriching life.

Reconnect with activities, hobbies, and interests that bring you joy. Have you always wanted to learn photography? Perhaps at school, you enjoyed dance but have lost it as an adult. Do you like hiking in the mountains? Now is the time to pick these things up again. Exploring your passions can help you rediscover a sense of purpose and fulfillment. Expand your social circle by meeting new people and forming new friendships. Engaging with different individuals can provide fresh perspectives and connections.

Consider exploring new places and cultures through travel. Traveling can be a transformative experience that broadens your horizons and provides a sense of adventure. If you cannot afford to travel, visit restaurants offering different cuisines or explore places around your city that you have never been to before. Pretend you're a tourist in your hometown. Where haven't you been?

Reflect on what you've learned from past relationships and apply those lessons to your future interactions. Use your experiences as stepping stones to personal growth.

Shift your mindset by practicing positive self-talk. Replace self-doubt with affirmations that empower and uplift you.

Embracing new opportunities and experiences after a breakup can empower you to lead a life filled with growth, positivity, and fulfillment. By taking intentional steps toward self-discovery and exploration, you're opening the door to a future that is rich with possibilities.

Closure: The Final Step in the Healing Process

Closure is a significant phase in the journey of moving on from a past relationship. It involves finding a sense of resolution, understanding, and acceptance that allows you to put the emotional baggage of the relationship behind you. Achieving closure can be essential for your emotional well-being and the start of a new chapter in your life. Here's how to navigate the path to closure after a breakup.

Reflect on Your Emotions

Take time to reflect on your emotions and acknowledge what you're feeling. Understand that it's normal to experience a range of emotions during this process.

Accept the Reality

Accept that the relationship has come to an end. Embrace the truth that seeking closure doesn't necessarily mean rekindling the relationship. Give yourself permission to grieve the loss of the relationship. Allow your emotions to flow naturally, whether it's sadness, anger, or even relief. You may need to remove the person's personal belongings from your home to help with this.

Communicate Your Feelings

If you feel the need, communicate your feelings to your ex-partner. Express your thoughts calmly and assertively, focusing on your own emotions rather than blaming others.

Seek Understanding

Seek understanding rather than blame. Try to understand both your perspective and your ex-partner's perspective on the relationship.

Let Go of Unanswered Questions

Accept that you may not get all the answers you're seeking. Let go of the need to have every question answered to find closure. While external conversations can contribute to closure, remember that closure is primarily an internal process. It's about finding peace within yourself.

Boundary Setting Worksheets

Setting healthy boundaries is crucial for maintaining positive relationships and protecting your well-being. Use these worksheets to help you identify, communicate, and maintain your boundaries effectively.

Identifying Your Boundaries Worksheet

Reflect on different areas of your life where you'd like to establish boundaries. Consider emotional, physical, and time-related boundaries. Write down specific situations and the boundaries you want to set.

Area of Life:

Emotional Boundaries:

Situation:

Boundary:

Situation:

Boundary:

Physical Boundaries:

Situation:

Boundary:

___

Situation:

___

Boundary:

___

Time-Related Boundaries:

Situation:

___

Boundary:

___

Situation:

___

Boundary:

___

Remember, boundaries are about respecting your needs and values and requiring others to do the same. Be specific about the situations you encounter and the boundaries you want to set to enhance your well-being and relationships.

Communicating Your Boundaries

Practice communicating your boundaries assertively and respectfully. Role-play different scenarios where you need to communicate your boundaries with friends, family, or colleagues.

Scenario 1:

Role-Player A:

Role-Player B:

Boundary to Communicate:

Assertive Communication Script:

Role-Player A: "Hey, I wanted to talk to you about something that's important to me. I've realized that I need to set a boundary around [specific situation] to [ensure my well-being, protect my time, etc.]. I hope you understand and respect my need for this boundary."

Role-Player B: "Thank you for letting me know. I appreciate your honesty, and I'll make sure to respect your boundaries."

Scenario 2:

Role-Player A:

Role-Player B:

Boundary to Communicate:

Assertive Communication Script:

Role-Player A: "I've been thinking about my boundaries lately, and I wanted to share something with you. When it comes to [specific situations], I've realized that I need to establish a boundary to [maintain my emotional well-being, balance my commitments, etc.]. I hope you understand where I'm coming from."

Role-Player B: "Thank you for telling me. I respect your need to set boundaries, and I'll do my best to support that."

Scenario 3:

Role-Player A:

_____

Role-Player B:

_____

Boundary to Communicate:

_____

Assertive Communication Script:

Role-Player A: "I value our relationship, and I want to have an open conversation about setting a boundary. When it comes to [a specific situation], I believe it's important for me to establish a boundary to [take care of myself, create a healthy work-life balance, etc.]. I hope we can find a way that works for both of us."

Role-Player B: "Thank you for bringing this up. Your well-being matters to me, and I'll make an effort to respect the boundary you're setting."

Remember, assertive communication involves being clear, respectful, and confident while expressing your boundaries. Practicing these scenarios can help you feel more prepared when real-life situations arise.

Remember that boundary-setting is an ongoing process, and these worksheets can serve as tools to help you navigate this journey effectively.

CHAPTER 8:
STOP BEING A TOXIC RELATIONSHIP MAGNET

A re you familiar with the feeling of being caught in a cycle of toxic relationships and unsure of how to break free? If so, you're not alone. This chapter is dedicated to those who are ready to break the pattern and create healthier connections. Recognizing toxic relationship dynamics can be challenging, but it's an essential step towards building the kind of relationships you truly deserve. In the following pages, we will explore the signs of toxic relationships, delve into the underlying factors that might attract you to them, and provide actionable strategies to help you steer clear of toxicity and cultivate connections that uplift and empower you. Remember, you have the power to break free from toxic relationship patterns and create a foundation for nurturing and fulfilling connections in your life.

Navigating the Dating Pool Again

Reentering the dating scene after experiencing toxic relationships can be both exciting and daunting. This section is designed to provide you with a step-by-step guide on how to venture into dating once more, armed with the knowledge and insights to avoid falling into toxic patterns. While it's important to take your time and heal before diving back in, the journey toward building healthy relationships can be immensely rewarding.

➢ **Give Yourself Time to Heal:** Before you embark on a new romantic journey, ensure you've given yourself enough time to heal from past wounds. Reflect on your past relationships, learn from them, and work on self-care and personal growth.

➢ **Recognize Your Readiness:** Assess your emotional state and determine whether you're truly ready to date again. Look for signs of emotional stability, self-awareness, and a willingness to engage in healthy interactions.

➢ **Set Clear Intentions:** Define what you're looking for in a relationship. Are you seeking companionship, a serious commitment, or something casual? Knowing your intentions will help you communicate your needs effectively.

➢ **Identify Red Flags:** Learn from your past experiences by identifying red flags that may have been present in toxic relationships. Be vigilant and trust your intuition when you encounter potential partners.

➢ **Take Your Time:** Avoid rushing into a new relationship. Take the time to get to know potential partners and build a foundation of trust and understanding.

➢ **Communicate Openly:** Practice open and honest communication from the start. Clearly express your boundaries, values, and expectations to ensure compatibility and mutual respect.

> **Trust Your Instincts:** Trust your gut feelings about a person and a relationship. If something doesn't feel right or resonates with your past experiences, don't ignore these feelings.

> **Seek Professional Support:** If you find yourself struggling with anxiety, self-doubt, or fears from past toxic relationships, consider seeking support from a therapist or counselor to help you navigate the dating world with confidence.

Remember, your journey toward healthier relationships is a process, and it's perfectly fine to take things at your own pace. The goal is to build connections that uplift and support you, helping you break free from the cycle of toxicity and creating a foundation for a more fulfilling romantic future.

How to Handle New Relationships

Entering a new relationship after a history of toxic connections can be scary. This section provides valuable insights and strategies to help you navigate the early stages of a new relationship with confidence and mindfulness, ensuring that you build a healthy and positive foundation.

> **Embrace Self-Awareness:** Before you immerse yourself in a new relationship, take time to reflect on your emotional state, triggers, and desires. Self-awareness will empower you to make conscious choices and communicate effectively.

> **Learn from Past Mistakes:** Acknowledge the lessons you've learned from past toxic relationships. Use these insights to set healthy boundaries, recognize red flags, and make better decisions moving forward.

➢ **Take Things Slowly:** Avoid rushing into deep commitments. Allow the relationship to evolve naturally, and give yourself time to assess compatibility and emotional safety.

➢ **Communicate Openly:** Open communication is essential in any healthy relationship. Express your feelings, concerns, and expectations honestly, and encourage your partner to do the same.

➢ **Trust Incrementally:** Trust needs to be earned over time. While it's important to be open, don't feel pressured to reveal all your vulnerabilities immediately. Gradually build trust as you get to know your partner better.

➢ **Set Clear Boundaries:** Clearly define your boundaries and communicate them to your partner. Healthy relationships thrive on mutual respect and understanding of each other's limits.

➢ **Prioritize Compatibility:** Look for compatibility in terms of values, interests, and life goals. A strong foundation of shared values can help sustain a healthy relationship.

➢ **Be Mindful of Red Flags:** Pay attention to any behaviors that trigger your past negative experiences. If you notice any red flags, address them openly and honestly, and decide whether the relationship is worth pursuing.

➢ **Seek Growth Together:** Healthy relationships encourage personal growth and mutual support. Focus on nurturing each other's aspirations and evolving together as a couple and separately as individuals.

> **Seek Professional Guidance:** If you find yourself struggling with trust issues, anxiety, or old wounds resurfacing, consider seeking guidance from a therapist or counselor to navigate your feelings and concerns.

> **Be Patient:** Building a healthy and lasting relationship takes time. Be patient with yourself and your partner as you learn and grow together.

Approaching new relationships with intention, mindfulness, and self-awareness can significantly increase your chances of breaking free from toxic patterns and fostering a fulfilling and loving connection.

Healthy vs Unhealthy Relationships

Recognizing the distinction between healthy and unhealthy relationships is vital for your emotional well-being and personal growth. Whether you're starting a new relationship or reevaluating an existing one, understanding the characteristics that define each type of relationship can empower you to make informed decisions and cultivate meaningful connections.

Healthy Relationships

Healthy relationships are built on mutual respect, communication, and a foundation of trust. Here are some key characteristics that define healthy relationships:

> **Respect and Equality:** Partners in a healthy relationship treat each other with respect, valuing each other's opinions, feelings, and boundaries. There is a sense of equality in decision-making and shared responsibilities.

➢ **Open Communication:** Effective communication is a cornerstone of healthy relationships. Partners actively listen, express their thoughts and feelings honestly, and address conflicts in a respectful and non-blaming manner.

➢ **Trust and Honesty:** Trust is established through consistent honesty, reliability, and transparency. Partners have faith in each other's words and actions.

➢ **Supportive Environment:** Healthy relationships provide emotional support, encouragement, and a safe space for each partner to express themselves without fear of judgment.

➢ **Independence:** Both partners maintain their individuality and personal interests, allowing each other space to grow and pursue their passions.

➢ **Shared Values:** Healthy relationships are grounded in shared values, goals, and aspirations. Partners are aligned in their life paths and support each other's growth.

➢ **Healthy Conflict Resolution:** Disagreements are addressed through open dialogue and compromise. Partners work together to find solutions that benefit both parties.

➢ **Personal Growth:** Healthy relationships encourage personal development and growth, enabling each partner to become the best version of themselves.

Unhealthy Relationships

Unhealthy relationships are characterized by imbalance, a lack of respect, and negative patterns. Here are signs of an unhealthy relationship:

➢ **Lack of Respect:** Partners disrespect each other's boundaries, opinions, and feelings. Disparaging comments and belittling behavior may be present.

➢ **Poor Communication:** Communication is strained, marked by misunderstandings, criticism, and avoidance of conflicts.

➢ **Lack of Trust:** Trust issues may arise due to dishonesty, secrecy, or betrayal. Partners may question each other's motives and intentions.

➢ **Isolation:** One partner may attempt to isolate the other from friends, family, or activities, exerting control and dominance.

➢ **Power Imbalance:** Power struggles, manipulation, and controlling behavior characterize unhealthy relationships.

➢ **Constant Criticism:** Partners criticize each other frequently, leading to feelings of inadequacy and low self-esteem.

➢ **Repeated Conflict:** Conflict is frequent and unresolved, with both partners feeling unheard and unvalidated.

➢ **Stagnation:** Unhealthy relationships hinder personal growth and may cause each partner to lose sight of their own goals and interests.

Understanding the differences between healthy and unhealthy relationships is crucial for your well-being. If you find yourself in an unhealthy relationship, consider seeking support from friends, family, or professionals to help you make informed decisions and create positive changes.

Building Healthy Relationships

Cultivating healthy relationships is a vital component of emotional well-being and personal fulfillment. Whether you're seeking to establish new connections or strengthen existing ones, the principles of healthy relationships remain constant. By focusing on mutual respect, effective communication, and shared values, you can foster supportive relationships, nurturing, and empowering.

Maintaining Healthy Boundaries for Future Relationships

Creating and sustaining healthy boundaries is a fundamental aspect of building and maintaining fulfilling relationships. Boundaries serve as guidelines that define your limits, needs, and expectations in any relationship. By setting and maintaining healthy boundaries, you ensure that your well-being and personal space are respected while also fostering open and respectful interactions with your partner.

Reflect on Your Boundaries

Take the time to reflect on your boundaries, both emotional and physical, based on your experiences and needs. Identify areas where you feel comfortable and areas where you might need to establish clearer boundaries in future relationships.

Communicate Early and Clearly

Open communication is key to setting and maintaining healthy boundaries. Communicate your boundaries early in a relationship, clearly expressing your needs and expectations. Effective communication helps avoid misunderstandings and allows both partners to be on the same page.

Stay Consistent

Consistency is essential when it comes to boundaries. Be sure to uphold the boundaries you set and avoid making exceptions that compromise your well-being. Consistency reinforces your commitment to self-respect and helps build a foundation of trust in the relationship.

Be Assertive

Assertiveness is about confidently expressing your needs while also respecting the needs of your partner. When communicating your boundaries, use "I" statements and focus on your feelings and needs rather than placing blame.

Respect Your Partner's Boundaries

Healthy boundaries are a two-way street. Just as you want your boundaries to be respected, make sure to respect your partner's boundaries as well. This mutual respect fosters a balanced and respectful relationship.

Reevaluate as Needed

As relationships evolve, it's important to reevaluate your boundaries. Changes in circumstances or personal growth may require adjustments to your boundaries. Regularly check in with yourself and your partner to ensure that your boundaries remain relevant and appropriate.

Trust Your Instincts

Your instincts can be a valuable guide when it comes to setting boundaries. If something doesn't feel right, trust your feelings, and take the necessary steps to establish boundaries that protect your emotional and physical well-being.

Maintaining healthy boundaries is an ongoing practice that requires self-awareness, effective communication, and a commitment to your well-being. By setting and respecting boundaries, you empower yourself to create relationships that are based on respect, trust, and mutual understanding.

Strategies for Effective Communication

Effective communication is the cornerstone of any healthy and thriving relationship. It involves both expressing your thoughts and feelings clearly and actively listening to your partner. By honing your communication skills, you can prevent misunderstandings, resolve conflicts, and foster deeper connections in your relationships.

- ➢ **Active Listening:** Practice active listening by giving your full attention to the speaker. Avoid interrupting and focus on understanding their perspective before formulating your response.

- ➢ **Use "I" Statements:** When discussing your feelings or concerns, use "I" statements to express your thoughts without blaming or accusing. This helps prevent defensiveness and encourages open dialogue.

- ➢ **Be Clear and Concise:** Communicate your message clearly and concisely. Avoid vague language and provide specific details to ensure that your partner understands your point of view.

- ➢ **Practice Empathy:** Put yourself in your partner's shoes to understand their feelings and perspective. Empathy demonstrates that you value their emotions and are open to understanding their viewpoint.

- ➢ **Avoid Negative Language:** Steer clear of negative language, criticism, or sarcasm. Focus on constructive communication that promotes understanding and respect. Phrases like, "You always…" or "You never…" are unhelpful.

➤ **Non-Verbal Communication:** Remember that non-verbal cues, such as facial expressions, gestures, and body language all play a crucial role in communication. Pay attention to these cues to gain a deeper understanding of what your partner is conveying.

➤ **Ask Open-Ended Questions:** Encourage meaningful conversations by asking open-ended questions that require more than a simple "yes" or "no" answer. These questions prompt your partner to share their thoughts and feelings.

➤ **Practice Patience:** Effective communication takes time, especially when discussing complex or emotional topics. Be patient and give your partner the space to express themselves fully without interruption.

➤ **Avoid Assumptions:** Avoid assuming that you know what your partner is thinking or feeling. Instead, ask for clarification and encourage them to express themselves openly.

➤ **Conflict Resolution:** When conflicts arise, approach them with a solution-oriented mindset. Focus on resolving the issue rather than assigning blame.

➤ **Manage Emotions:** Stay composed and avoid reacting impulsively, especially during heated discussions. Take a moment to manage your emotions before responding.

➤ Reflective Listening: Reflect back on what you've heard to ensure that you've understood your partner correctly. This shows that you value their perspective and encourage them to elaborate if needed.

Effective communication is an ongoing practice that requires intention, patience, and self-awareness. By employing these strategies, you can create an environment of open dialogue, trust, and understanding in your relationships.

Effective Communication Worksheets

Enhancing your communication skills is a valuable endeavor that can greatly improve your relationships. These worksheets provide exercises and activities to help you practice and refine your communication abilities, allowing you to engage in more meaningful and productive interactions.

Reflective Listening Exercise

Reflective listening is a valuable skill that fosters effective communication and understanding. Practice this skill by engaging in the following exercises: In each scenario, paraphrase what the speaker has said to demonstrate your comprehension and encourage open dialogue.

Scenario 1: Work Setting

Imagine you're in a team meeting, and a colleague expresses concerns about a project's timeline.

Speaker's Statement: "I'm worried that we might not meet the project deadline because we're facing unexpected challenges."

Your Reflective Response:

_____

_____

_____

Scenario 2: Personal Conversation

You're having a conversation with a friend who is sharing their excitement about a new opportunity.

Speaker's Statement: "I can't believe I got the job offer! It's such an amazing opportunity, and I'm thrilled about the possibilities."

Your Reflective Response:

_____

_____

_____

Scenario 3: Family Gathering

During a family gathering, your sibling talks about feeling overwhelmed with their responsibilities.

Speaker's Statement: "I've been juggling work, kids, and household chores, and it's been tough to keep up with everything."

Your Reflective Response:

_____

_____

_____

Scenario 4: Social Event

At a social event, someone discusses their recent travel experiences and the challenges they encountered.

Speaker's Statement: "The trip was incredible, but dealing with the language barrier was a bit frustrating at times."

Your Reflective Response:

_____

_____

_____

Scenario 5: Educational Setting

In a classroom discussion, a classmate shares their perspective on a complex topic.

Speaker's Statement: "I believe that incorporating sustainable practices into our daily lives is crucial for a better future."

Your Reflective Response:

_____

_____

_____

Practicing reflective listening enhances your ability to connect with others, demonstrates empathy, and fosters effective communication. Use this exercise to refine your reflective listening skills in various contexts, promoting meaningful interactions.

Non-Verbal Communication Awareness Worksheet

Non-verbal communication, including gestures, facial expressions, body language, and tone of voice, often conveys more than words alone. Use this worksheet to enhance your awareness of non-verbal cues in various situations. Observe and analyze the non-verbal signals in each scenario to develop a deeper understanding of the unspoken aspects of communication.

Scenario 1: Job Interview

Imagine you're conducting a job interview. Pay attention to the non-verbal cues exhibited by the interviewee and interviewer.

➢ **Interviewee's Non-Verbal Cues:**

- Facial expressions:

  _____

- Body language:

  _____

- Eye contact:

  _____

- Tone of voice:

  _____

➢ **Interviewer's Non-Verbal Cues:**

- Facial expressions:

  _____

- Body language:

  _____

- Eye contact:

  _____

- Tone of voice:

  _____

Scenario 2: Social Gathering

Visualize a social gathering where people are engaged in conversations. Observe the non-verbal cues among individuals.

➤ **Person A's Non-Verbal Cues:**

- Facial expressions:

  _____

- Body language:

  _____

- Eye contact:

  _____

- Tone of voice:

  _____

➤ **Person B's Non-Verbal Cues:**

- Facial expressions:

  _____

- Body language:

  _____

- Eye contact:

  _____

- Tone of voice:

  _____

Open-Ended Question Exercise Worksheet

Open-ended questions are powerful tools for sparking meaningful conversations and gaining insights into others' thoughts and feelings. Use this worksheet to create open-ended questions that can lead to deeper and more engaging dialogues with your partner, friends, or family members.

1. Conversation Partner:

Who would you like to have a meaningful conversation with? (Partner, friend, family member, etc.)

_____

2. Choose a Topic:

Select a topic or area of discussion that you'd like to explore in depth. (e.g., relationships, personal growth, hobbies, goals, etc.)

_____

3. Create Open-Ended Questions:

Generate open-ended questions related to the chosen topic. These questions should encourage your conversation partner to share their thoughts, feelings, and insights. Remember to avoid questions that can be answered with a simple "yes" or "no."

Topic: _____

What are your thoughts about [topic]?

_____

How does [topic] impact your life?

_____

Can you share an experience that relates to [topic]?

_____

What emotions do you associate with [topic]?

_____

What do you find most interesting or challenging about [topic]?

_____

How has your perspective on [topic] evolved?

_____

What role does [topic] play in your future plans or goals?

_____

Can you describe a moment when [topic] made a significant impact on you?

_____

How do you think [topic] influences your relationships?

_____

What do you think others often misunderstand about [topic]?

_____

4. Conversation Reflection:

Consider the potential impact of these open-ended questions on your conversations. How might they lead to deeper discussions and a better understanding of your conversation partner?

---

5. Plan Your Conversation:

Choose a time and setting that are conducive to a meaningful conversation. Approach the conversation with curiosity and a genuine desire to listen and learn from your partner's responses.

These worksheets are designed to support your journey towards better communication skills. Regular practice of these exercises will contribute to more fulfilling and harmonious relationships in various aspects of your life.

Healthy Relationships Worksheets

Nurturing healthy relationships is a vital aspect of a fulfilling life. These worksheets offer a range of activities and exercises to help you cultivate and maintain strong, positive, and respectful relationships with those around you.

Relationship Values Reflection Worksheet

Understanding your core values in relationships is essential for building healthy and fulfilling connections. This worksheet will help you identify and reflect on the values that you prioritize in your relationships.

1. Self-Reflection:

Take a moment to think about your past relationships and what aspects of them were most important to you. Consider the qualities that made those relationships meaningful and satisfying.

_____

_____

_____

2. Identify Core Values:

Review the list of common relationship values below. Circle or highlight the values that resonate with you the most. Feel free to add any values that aren't listed.

- ➤ Trust
- ➤ Communication
- ➤ Respect
- ➤ Honesty
- ➤ Empathy
- ➤ Support
- ➤ Equality
- ➤ Vulnerability
- ➤ Independence
- ➤ Shared Goals
- ➤ Quality Time
- ➤ Loyalty
- ➤ Open-mindedness
- ➤ Growth
- ➤ Playfulness

_____

_____

_____

3. Reflect on Your Choices:

For each value you've selected, take a moment to reflect on why it's important to you in a relationship. Consider how it contributes to your overall well-being and the health of your connections.

_____

_____

_____

4. Prioritize Your Values:

Rank the values you've selected in order of importance to you. Begin with the value that holds the most significance and continue until you've ranked all of them.

4. _____

5. _____

6. _____

7. _____

8. _____

5. Real-Life Application:

Think about how these values have influenced your past relationships or interactions. Were there times when your values aligned well with your

STOP BEING A TOXIC RELATIONSHIP MAGNET

partner's, and times when they didn't? How did those experiences impact the relationship's quality?

_____

_____

_____

6. Goal Setting:

Consider how you can incorporate these values into your current or future relationships. Are there specific actions you can take to align your relationships with your core values?

_____

_____

_____

7. Reflection:

Take a moment to reflect on the insights gained from this exercise. How can understanding your core values help you build and maintain healthier and more fulfilling relationships in the future?

_____

_____

_____

Communication Styles Assessment Worksheet

Effective communication is essential for building and maintaining healthy relationships. This worksheet will help you assess your current communication style and explore strategies for enhancing your communication skills.

1. Self-Assessment:

Read the following statements and circle the number that best represents how frequently each statement describes your communication style. Use the following scale:

1 = Rarely 2 = Sometimes 3 = Often 4 = Almost Always

1. I actively listen to others without interrupting them. (1, 2, 3, 4)

2. I express my thoughts and feelings clearly and confidently. (1, 2, 3, 4)

3. I am attentive to non-verbal cues like body language and facial expressions. (1, 2, 3, 4)

4. I ask open-ended questions to encourage deeper conversations. (1, 2, 3, 4)

5. I am patient and willing to listen, even when I disagree with the speaker. (1, 2, 3, 4)

6. I tend to dominate conversations and talk more than I listen. (1, 2, 3, 4)

7. I avoid discussing my emotions or thoughts to prevent conflict. (1, 2, 3, 4)

8. I struggle to express my needs or concerns to others. (1, 2, 3, 4)

9. I become defensive when receiving feedback or criticism. (1, 2, 3, 4)

10. I am aware of the impact of my words and tone on others. (1, 2, 3, 4)

2. Assessing Your Style:

Add up the scores for each set of statements to identify your communication style tendencies:

Active Listening: Statements 1 + 3 + 5 + 10 =

_____

Assertive Expression: Statements 2 + 4 =

_____

Passive Communication: Statements 7 + 8 =

_____

Defensive Communication: Statements 6 + 9 =

_____

3. Reflecting on Your Style:

Take a moment to reflect on your communication style tendencies. Which style do you find yourself using most often? Are there any styles that you would like to improve or change?

_____

_____

_____

4. Strategies for Improvement:

For each style, consider one strategy you could implement to enhance your communication skills:

Active Listening:

Assertive Expression:

_____

Passive Communication:

_____

Defensive Communication:

_____

5. Action Plan:

Select one strategy that you would like to focus on improving. Outline steps you can take to incorporate this strategy into your daily interactions.

_____

_____

_____

_____

6. Reflection:

Reflect on how being more aware of your communication style and implementing these strategies can positively impact your relationships. What changes do you hope to see in your interactions with others?

_____

_____

_____

_____

Conflict Resolution Strategies Worksheet

Conflict is a normal part of relationships, and how we address it can greatly impact their health and longevity. This worksheet will help you explore and practice conflict resolution strategies for handling disagreements healthily and productively.

1. Understanding Conflict:

Define the conflict or disagreement you are currently facing:

_____

_____

_____

2. Emotions and Reactions:

Identify your emotional reactions to the conflict:

_____

_____

_____

3. Choose Your Approach:

Read through the conflict resolution strategies below and choose one that you believe would be most effective for your current situation.

> ➤ Collaboration: Working together to find a mutually beneficial solution.

> ➤ Compromise: Finding a middle ground where both parties give and take.

> ➤ Assertion: Expressing your needs and opinions while respecting others.

> ➤ Active Listening: Listening attentively to the other person's perspective.

> ➤ Problem-Solving: Identifying the root cause and jointly finding solutions.

4. Strategy Implementation:

Describe how you can apply your chosen conflict resolution strategy to address the current conflict:

_____

_____

_____

5. Active Listening Practice:

Write down three open-ended questions you can ask to better understand the other person's perspective:

1. _____

2. _____

3. _____

6. Self-Reflection:

Consider the following questions and write down your responses:

> ➤ How did your chosen strategy influence the conflict resolution process?

➢ Were there any challenges you encountered while applying the strategy?

➢ What positive outcomes or insights did you gain from using this approach?

7. Future Conflict Resolution:

Think about how you can incorporate the strategies you've learned into your future conflict-resolution efforts. Write down one goal for enhancing your conflict resolution skills:

8. Conclusion:

Reflect on the importance of resolving conflicts healthily and productively for maintaining positive relationships.

Healthy Relationship Quiz

Assess the health of your relationships with this quiz. Reflect on various aspects of your relationships to identify areas for improvement and growth.

Instructions:

For each question, rate your response on a scale of 1 to 5, where 1 represents "Strongly Disagree" and 5 represents "Strongly Agree." Be honest in your assessment to gain insights into your relationships.

1. Communication:

1. I feel comfortable expressing my thoughts and feelings to my partner/friend.

   _____

2. My partner/friend actively listens to me and shows genuine interest in what I say.

   _____

3. We openly discuss problems and conflicts, seeking solutions together.

   _____

2. Trust and Honesty:

1. I trust my partner/friend to be truthful and transparent with me.

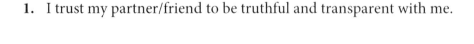

2. We both feel secure sharing our vulnerabilities without fear of judgment.

3. Our actions consistently match our words, fostering trust between us.

3. Respect:

1. We respect each other's boundaries and personal space.

2. Disagreements are handled respectfully, without belittling or demeaning each other.

3. Our opinions and choices are valued and considered by each other.

4. Support and Empathy:

1. We offer emotional support to each other during both good times and challenges.

2. My partner/friend shows empathy and understanding when I'm going through a tough time.

3. We celebrate each other's successes and achievements.

5. Equality and Balance:

1. Responsibilities and decisions are shared fairly in our relationship.

2. We both have an equal say in matters that affect us as a couple/friends.

3. Our relationship brings a sense of balance and enrichment to both of our lives.

Scoring:

Add up your scores for each question to get a total score of 75.

➤ 15–30: Your relationship may need significant improvement.

➤ 31–45: There are some positive aspects but room for growth.

➤ 46–60: Your relationship is generally healthy, with areas to focus on.

➤ 61–75: Your relationship is strong and thriving.

Reflection:

Review your total score and reflect on specific areas where you want to invest effort to enhance the health of your relationships. Remember that healthy relationships require ongoing care and communication.

_____

_____

_____

These worksheets are designed to enhance your understanding of healthy relationships and provide practical tools for nurturing them. Regular use of these exercises can contribute to the creation of meaningful and harmonious connections with the people in your life.

CONCLUSION

An this comprehensive guide, we've embarked on a journey to heal from broken relationships, transform our existing relationships, and empower ourselves with the knowledge and skills needed for healthy connections. From understanding toxic patterns to cultivating effective communication and conflict resolution, we've explored every facet of building and nurturing meaningful relationships.

The core message of this book is that healthy relationships are within your reach. Armed with self-awareness, effective communication, and boundary-setting skills, you have the power to create connections that uplift, support, and bring joy to your life. Remember that growth is a continuous process, and every effort you invest in your relationships will yield invaluable rewards.

Now that you're equipped with these invaluable tools, it's time to step out into the world and put them into practice. Whether it's fostering healthy boundaries, practicing open communication, or seeking shared values, embrace every opportunity to strengthen your relationships. Take your newfound knowledge and form new, enriched connections, one step at a time.

If you've found value in this book, I encourage you to share your experience by leaving a review on Amazon. Your feedback can inspire others to seek and build healthy relationships. Thank you for joining me on this transformative exploration, and remember, your relationships can become a source of genuine happiness and fulfillment.

ABOUT THE AUTHOR

Dylan Walker is an author and publishing entrepreneur. He lives in California with his wife and three children. He is passionate about health, wellness, simple living, and minimalism.

Dylan has spent many years focusing on healthy relationships, personal growth, and how to manage stress. His aim in writing these books is to help people reach their fullest potential with scientifically proven practices and to empower people from all backgrounds to improve their mental and physical well-being.

His mission is to help as many people as possible by sharing his comprehensive knowledge about living a physically and emotionally healthy lifestyle and forming and maintaining meaningful relationships.

You will enjoy Dylan's practical books if you are committed to improving your life for the long term.

THANK YOU

Thank you so much for purchasing this book.

You could have picked from dozens of other books but you took a chance and chose this one.

So THANK YOU for getting this book and for reading it all the way to the end.

Before you go, I wanted to ask you for one small favor. **Could you please consider posting a review on Amazon? Posting a review is the best and easiest way to support the work of independent authors like me.**

Your feedback will also help me to keep writing the kind of books that will help you get the results you want. It would mean a lot to me to hear from you.

>> Leave a review on Amazon US <<

>> Leave a review on Amazon UK <<

REFERENCES

A journey of self-discovery: Finding your true self and visualizing success. (2023, January 11). Psychic Source. https://www.psychicsource .com/article/health-wellness/a-journey-of-self-discovery-finding-your-true-self-and-visualizing-success/22171&ved=2ah UKEwjA1tjI1b3-AhWTtqQKHTw4AN04ChAWegQIB RAB&usg=AOvVaw1AfTfEEXlqIL5a_cgWY13j

AB. (2021, July 12). *7 amazing self-esteem worksheets.* Mixed in Beautiful. https://mixedinbeautiful.com/self-esteem-worksheets/&ved=2a hUKEwid2pSm1b3-AhWFMewKHUiYCmg4ChAWeg QIBxAB&usg=AOvVaw0yIabqEnVisLeum-BkKHQD

After a breakup how did you achieve your goals. (n.d.). Quora. https://www.quora.com/After-a-breakup-how-did-you-achieve-your-goals&ved=2ahUKEwiWuuvXo73-AhVN_KQKHQ9rDgE Qjjh6BAhEEAE&usg=AOvVaw10LXJgly9SVIhDidfqhUMN

Anne, D. (n.d.). *How to stop holding on to a relationship that's over.* Love Panky. https://www.lovepanky.com/love-couch/broken-heart/how-to-stop-holding-on-to-a-relationship-thats-over&ved=2ahUKEwi-2Lfmor3-AhVN3qQKHV1zD5AQFn oECA0QAQ&usg=AOvVaw3Kt8sWerSR7EOjHX5_38ia

Avila, L. (2021, January 9). *5 ways to heal from A breakup with mindfulness.* Your Tango. https://www.yourtango.com/experts/ lianne-avila/how-get-over-breakup-with-mindfulness%3 Famp&ved=2ahUKEwjp0YOrz73-AhUNH-wKHcf7B444Ch AWegQICBAB&usg=AOvVaw3MSsvtR4ysbEnt-VV4Ldtn

Backes, B. (n.d.). *Your feelings are valid, and other thoughts on emotional support.* Beth Backes. https://bethbackes.com/your- feelings-are-valid/amp/&ved=2ahUKEwjtrOTE0L3- AhWC5KQKHSaAASg4ChAWegQIBBAB&usg=AOvVaw0n8 m3nFUlMLgqvbz8y3Wwb

Baer, D. (2017, February 17). *Heartbreak looks a lot like drug withdrawal in the brain.* The Cut. https://www.thecut.com/ 2017/02/why-heartbreak-getting-dumped-feel-so-bad.html

Bailey, K. (2018, July 31). *5 powerful health benefits of journaling.* Inter Mountain Health Care. https://intermountainhealthcare.org/ blogs/topics/live-well/2018/07/5-powerful-health-benefits-of- journaling/&ved=2ahUKEwjTnrjb0b3-AhULPuwKHXb2B lIQFnoECBkQAQ&usg=AOvVaw24UhJr5pXIjlGE0dWMeQ9R

Boundaries circle worksheet (PDF download). (n.d.). Ineffable Living. https://ineffableliving.com/boundaries-circle-worksheet-pdf- download/&ved=2ahUKEwiq3eeHpb3-AhVEy6QKHXlYD844F BAWegQICBAB&usg=AOvVaw0uFFfFBbIJ-Njjr13wmDkB

Bridges, F. (2017, June 21). *10 ways to build confidence.* Forbes. https://www.forbes.com/sites/francesbridges/2017/07/21/10- ways-to-build-confidence/%3Fsh%3D783c50843c59&ved= 2ahUKEwiFvorv073-AhWE-KQKHdDwCaIQFnoECD YQAQ&usg=AOvVaw3Ko4d-gPAuwG7DlEgou9P-

Bubert, L. (2021, March 31). *Burdened by low self-esteem? Here's how to lighten the load.* Greatist. https://greatist.com/grow/low-self-esteem&ved=2ahUKEwiN6K_B073-AhWmOOwKHdk1D9s4ChAWegQICxAB&usg=AOvVaw0yx9T6t8_KYODtNQD0gayv

Building and maintaining healthy relationships. (n.d.). Health Direct. https://www.healthdirect.gov.au/amp/article/building-and-maintaining-healthy-relationships&ved=2ahUKEwjghcePob3-AhXPFOwKHXtmDS0QFnoECDEQAQ&usg=AOvVaw2e976ZwI_YiLMjHNWbFP18

Celestine, N. (2021, September 10). *How to improve communication skills: 14 best worksheets.* Positive Psychology. https://positive psychology.com/how-to-improve-communication-skills/&ved=2ahUKEwih4M-qor3-AhWFDOwKHcSABwEQFnoECB0QAQ&usg=AOvVaw0GIkVFOgm3dty0J1C06Q_i

Characteristics of healthy & unhealthy relationships. (n.d.). Youth. https://youth.gov/youth-topics/teen-dating-violence/characteristics&ved=2ahUKEwjG9aTkoL3-AhXJsKQKHc1QC7QQFnoECCMQAQ&usg=AOvVaw3UbG4NoRGzyo3pD2byQ-xY

Cherry, K. (2023, February 13). *11 signs of low self-esteem.* Very Well Mind. https://www.verywellmind.com/signs-of-low-self-esteem-5185978&ved=2ahUKEwix9aCz073-AhWkOOwKHb1VatkQFnoECCgQAQ&usg=AOvVaw1_AmH8BAutCBxdPYft21or

Communication worksheets. (n.d.). English Worksheets Land. https://www.englishworksheetsland.com/communication.html&ved=2ahUKEwih4M-qor3-AhWFDOwKHcSABwEQFnoECBkQAQ&usg=AOvVaw2dk05y4AWgGx4oiW9Oc581

Coping strategies for better mental health. (2018). MediCentres.
https://www.medicentres.com/2018/11/coping-strategies-mental-
health/&ved=2ahUKEwiG6IDb0L3-AhXHNOwKHVKbCRMQ
FnoECBcQAQ&usg=AOvVaw1C1jejJj2XV370qVmlyjgt

Daskal, L. (2023, August 11). *19 simple ways to boost your self-esteem
quickly.* Inc. https://www.inc.com/lolly-daskal/19-simple-ways-
to-boost-your-self-esteem-quickly.html&ved=2ahUKEwjryPj
N073-AhUQuaQKHYrcBE0QFnoECCsQAQ&usg=Aov
Vaw1CotX8yA4jqxBj6M1zE1v-

Davenport, B. (n.d.). *If you're trying to be friends with your ex, remember
these 11 boundaries.* Live Bold and Bloom. https://liveboldand
bloom.com/05/relationships/boundaries-friends-ex&ved=2ahUK
EwiT3KL1o73-AhVtMewKHXUjCmMQFnoECCcQAQ&usg=
AOvVaw1fWWfsCBbQi-_JSXm1DQAz

Davenport, B. (2022, May 21). *21 examples of healthy boundaries in
relationships.* Live Bold and Bloom. https://liveboldandbloom
.com/05/relationships/healthy-boundaries-in-relationships
&ved=2ahUKEwiUk_Ckob3-AhUhMuwKHWqvAgMQFnoEC
FYQAQ&usg=AOvVaw3TvbQaxmWYsvwSR7FG1pON

Deschene, L. (n.d.). *Tiny wisdom: Your feelings are real and valid.* Tiny
Buddha. https://tinybuddha.com/quotes/tiny-wisdom-your-
feelings-are-real-and-valid/&ved=2ahUKEwiO1a200L3-
AhUKtaQKHfFPDNQQFnoECCYQAQ&usg=AOvVaw0XUfB
XtXe9Mfgr7xaniC3a

Developing your support system. (n.d.). University of Buffalo.
https://socialwork.buffalo.edu/resources/self-care-starter-
kit/additional-self-care-resources/developing-your-support-

system.html&ved=2ahUKEwjEoLWU0r3-AhUlMewKHX9mBv
0QFnoECB0QAQ&usg=AOvVaw0svoo4p1xGg35KELtFBBno

E. Ackermann, C. (2017, May 23). *15 best self-esteem worksheets and
activities (incl. PDF).* Postive Psychology. https://positivepsycho
logy.com/self-esteem-worksheets/&ved=2ahUKEwjy0_OT1b3-
AhULHewKHYbaAVkQFnoECB8QAQ&usg=AOvVaw1Cx9BZ
WOo6xSNAlXrbk7Ph

Escamilla, S. (2022, February 15). *Your relationship is over — here's how
to stop holding onto it.* Bolde. https://www.bolde.com/your-
relationship-is-over-heres-how-to-stop-holding-onto-
it/&ved=2ahUKEwi-2Lfmor3-AhVN3qQKHV1zD5AQFnoECC
kQAQ&usg=AOvVaw21c1nPTlKmB1mRLyaWp1Ag

Femina. (2019, January 19). *Tips on starting a new relationship right after a
breakup.* Femina. https://m.femina.in/relationships/love-sex/tips-
on-starting-a-new-relationship-right-after-a-breakup-115259.
amp&ved=2ahUKEwil6bOioL3-AhUIxQIHHSXJDWIQ
FnoECA0QAQ&usg=AOvVaw0GqPZQw2UYNj40gBRZh2zN

Ferrante, C. (2021, November 11). *6 psychologist-backed ways to move
on after a breakup.* The Every Girl. https://theeverygirl.com/
psychologist-how-to-move-on-after-a-breakup/&ved=2ahUK
EwjC4J_Eo73-AhWIjaQKHURhAikQFnoECCwQAQ&usg=A
OvVaw3DO84gaNEJy_h6cjU1fF29

Field, B. (2022, December 11). *How to start dating after A breakup.*
Very Well Mind. http://www.verywellmind.com/how-to-start-
dating-after-a-breakup-6741121&ved=2ahUKEwjh0ueEoL3-
AhUCzqQKHf0lBxcQFnoECAsQBQ&usg=AOvVaw2p0i6P-
vEvLMNydb7j5yN0

Fielding, S. (2022, September 23). *7 signs of a toxic relationship and what to do to fix it, according to couple therapists.* Insider. https://www.insider.com/guides/health/mental-health/toxic-relationship%3Famp&ved=2ahUKEwjssMWRor3-AhVpMewKHecZCJcQFnoECCYQAQ&usg=AOvVaw0yR4qoGhe9Bn0uLWqGYM21

Fight, flight, freeze, fawn and flop: Response to trauma. (2021, November 15). APN. https://apn.com/resources/fight-flight-freeze-fawn-and-flop-responses-to-trauma/%23:~:text%3DThe%2520flight%2520trauma%2520response%2520involves

Fisher, H. (2023, February 7). *In the brain, romantic love is basically an addiction.* Discover. https://www.discovermagazine.com/mind/in-the-brain-romantic-love-is-basically-an-addiction&ved=2ahUKEwjs7JDznL3-AhWTraQKHQqzD48QFnoECCoQAQ&usg=AOvVaw2gcbRqVdVSeSPbY-4f_hYc

Friedmann, W. J. (n.d.). *Feelings are authentic and valid — perceptions and beliefs are suspect.* Mental Help. https://www.mentalhelp.net/blogs/feelings-are-authentic-and-valid-perceptions-and-beliefs-are-suspect/&ved=2ahUKEwiO1a200L3-AhUKtaQKHfFPDNQQFnoECCEQAQ&usg=AOvVaw2dBOwqLbXG5C5nCa6Y-IT4

Galanos, S. (2017, December 13). *A therapist's advice on getting over heartbreak.* Shaun Galanos Medium. https://shaungalanos.medium.com/a-therapists-how-to-on-getting-over-your-brutal-breakup-c43e9355be8d&ved=2ahUKEwi26arPzr3-AhXCwQIHHQlYAVs4HhAWegQIBBAB&usg=AOvVaw2MSlHSDp_SVJ0gwIOBJKwu

Get over your breakup by setting goals. (n.d.). Get Back My Ex. https://getbackmyex.com/advice/get-over-breakup-by-setting-goals/&ved=2ahUKEwiWuuvXo73-AhVN_KQKHQ9rDgEQFnoECCgQAQ&usg=AOvVaw288pww1RbHSU0_2bWakHOU

Getting started with mindfulness. (n.d.). Mindful. https://www.mindful.org/meditation/mindfulness-getting-started/

Gonzalez, A. (2023, January 6). *Healthy vs. unhealthy relationships.* WebMd. https://www.webmd.com/sex-relationships/healthy-vs-unhealthy-relationships&ved=2ahUKEwjG9aTkoL3-AhXJsKQKHc1QC7QQFnoECCgQAQ&usg=AOvVaw1eRNLlDcyAg2nwhe5iLcjn

Goop. (2021, March 18). *Why the post-breakup period can be surprisingly powerful.* Goop. https://goop.com/wellness/relationships/how-to-handle-a-breakup/&ved=2ahUKEwjNmrmwpL3-AhWQOewKHWG3AEA4HhAWegQIBBAB&usg=AOvVaw1br8EzKTL2G-mXxUY_hVf7

Griffin, T. (2023, August 17). *How to be strong after a breakup.* WikiHow. https://www.wikihow.com/Be-Strong-After-a-Breakup&ved=2ahUKEwjgteiH1L3-AhUpuaQKHQkvCokQFnoECBoQAQ&usg=AOvVaw1CUGz6MBp2FdxCNuLo0T0q

Habash, C. (n.d.). *What is self-reflection? Why is self-reflection important?* Thrive Works. https://thriveworks.com/blog/importance-self-reflection-improvement/%23:~:text%3DSelf%252Dreflection%2520is%2520the%2520key

HACEY. (2021, August 27). *Heartbreaks & mental health.* HACEY. https://hacey.org/health/heartbreaks-mental-health/&ved=2ahUKEwjh4PO0zL3-AhWIjaQKHTmOAvQQFnoECAkQAQ&usg=AOvVaw1NFerLzGrC6X2_f0KYm8OX

Harper, C. (n.d.). *Three ways to build a support system.* My Wellbeing. https://mywellbeing.com/therapy-101/how-to-build-a-support-system&ved=2ahUKEwjEoLWU0r3-AhUlMewKHX9mBv0 QFnoECB4QAQ&usg=AOvVaw2sFue8rzx9I5KguFw9yduP

Hay, L. (n.d.). *The power of affirmations.* Louise Hay. https://www.lo uisehay.com/the-power-of-affirmations/&ved=2ahUKEwjF99-n0b3-AhUPJewKHQcyD2UQFnoECFUQAQ&usg=AovVa w287SPe8Q0FgMG5qhC6a6Iw

Healthy coping strategies for mental health. (n.d.). Rose Hill Center. https://www.rosehillcenter.org/mental-health-blog/healthy-coping-strategies-for-mental-health/&ved=2ahUKEwiG6ID b0L3-AhXHNOwKHVKbCRMQFnoECB0QAQ&usg=A OvVaw1gR2yswQ8TCQnNyoZ4rkH8

Healthy relationships worksheets. (2023a). Care Patron. https://www.ca repatron.com/templates/healthy-relationships-worksheets &ved=2ahUKEwiEh_nDor3-AhUKrKQKHUj9BB4QFnoECBw QAQ&usg=AOvVaw0cGA_Y2jteoA9ETb4ApUfL

Healthy relationships worksheets. (2023b). The Wellness Society. https://thewellnesssociety.org/healthy-relationships-workshe ets-pdf/&ved=2ahUKEwiEh_nDor3-AhUKrKQKHUj9BB4 QFnoECB4QAQ&usg=AOvVaw3t0SPBmKN4Xgxb-XfLuBTI

Healthy vs. unhealthy relationships. (n.d.). Study. https://study.com/ learn/lesson/healthy-vs-unhealthy-relationships-characteristics-differences-signs.html&ved=2ahUKEwjG9aTkoL3-AhXJsK QKHc1QC7QQFnoECCcQAQ&usg=AOvVaw0FoywxepBVOA sOT_Ar49TD

Horkovska, I. (n.d.). *How can therapy worksheets benefit your mental well-being?* Calmerry Blog. https://us.calmerry.com/blog/therapy/how-can-therapy-worksheets-benefit-your-mental-well-being/&ved=2ahUKEwjXhKPfz73-AhVK-aQKHdu_Dno4FBAWegQICBAB&usg=AOvVaw1kcBjoXqsjf_l8EA2eJkZw

How therapy can help people who have gone through a relationship breakup. (2021, December 27). Health for Life. https://healthforlifegr.com/how-therapy-can-help-people-who-have-gone-through-a-relationship-breakup/&ved=2ahUKEwikkfWXzr3-AhVJyKQKHQ0ACj44ChAWegQIAhAB&usg=AOvVaw3G48ip0nbXUIg4Yt2GXGdG

How to build self-confidence. (n.d.). Reach Out. https://au.reachout.com/articles/how-to-build-self-confidence&ved=2ahUKEwiFvorv073-AhWE-KQKHdDwCaIQFnoECBQQBQ&usg=AOvVaw2r0GQUR4_e7euRDItoAvPM

How to get over a breakup: 5 ways to move on. (n.d.). NBC News. https://www.nbcnews.com/better/amp/ncna968396&ved=2ahUKEwjC4J_Eo73-AhWIjaQKHUrhAikQFnoECA0QBQ&usg=AOvVaw0i0NL3BbAp__fIfRlrLRW1

How to set healthy boundaries in your relationship. (2020, September 3). Eugene Therapy. https://eugenetherapy.com/article/how-to-set-healthy-boundaries-in-your-relationship/&ved=2ahUKEwiUk_Ckob3-AhUhMuwKHWqvAgMQFnoECAwQBQ&usg=AOvVaw24KlsiMFjfFDITmmOMwfD9

Hughes, J. (n.d.). *Finally letting go of the pain and moving on after a breakup.* Tiny Buddha. https://tinybuddha.com/blog/finally-

letting-go-of-the-pain-moving-on-after-a-break-up/&ved=2ah
UKEwith4GBo73-AhVPhqQKHdKqBd8QFnoECC4QAQ
&usg=AOvVaw2Otj-pP3dxzvsXQUaiziXC

Ibey, E. (n.d.-a). *A 7-step plan for finding love after a devastating
breakup.* Tiny Buddha. https://tinybuddha.com/blog/a-7-step-
plan-for-finding-love-after-a-devastating-breakup/&ved=
2ahUKEwi32aPQoL3-AhV7xAIHHbBlBGE4KBAWegQIGB
AB&usg=AOvVaw3bGVDCy2nHXD9PeLmyC4bC

Ibey, E. (n.d.-b). *When you reframe your breakup as an opportunity,
everything changes.* Tiny Buddha. https://tinybuddha.com/blog/
when-you-reframe-your-breakup-as-an-opportunity-everything-
changes/&ved=2ahUKEwizt-eWpL3-AhWQ_qQKHdoxAi
AQFnoECA8QAQ&usg=AOvVaw0_3qR5UPnq2zoBQzO_tNla

Important boundaries of self-love you NEED after a breakup. (n.d.). The
Mrsing Link. https://themrsinglink.com/blog/important-
boundaries-of-self-love-you-need-after-a-breakup/&ved=2ah
UKEwiT3KL1o73-AhVtMewKHXUjCmMQFnoECCgQAQ
&usg=AOvVaw3mvgWGLvqmLr8dCtDl1PLT

Jash, T. (2020, January 15). *My break-up was controlling my life until I
took these steps.* AMP. https://amp.abc.net.au/article/everyday/
11787694&ved=2ahUKEwiIs7GspL3-AhXJsKQKHc1QC7Q4F
BAWegQIAxAB&usg=AOvVaw1uy9aKsmSSE0NEd4qKeA62

Journal prompts to get over a breakup. (n.d.). Seeking Serotonin.
https://seekingserotonin.com/journal-prompts-for-breakups/
&ved=2ahUKEwjRtPmE0r3-AhVEMewKHTgABpwQFn
oECCEQAQ&usg=AOvVaw2zTTnZjmopZNyJNsM21XlN

Journal prompts to heal a broken heart. (2022, January 4). Hope Therapy Center. https://hope-therapy-center.com/single-post/2022/01/04-journal-prompts-to-heal-a-broken-heart/&ved=2ahUKEwjRtPm E0r3-AhVEMewKHTgABpwQFnoECA4QBQ&usg=AOvVaw1-Gq2Gms7N5Z1C0H40DTRj

Journaling prompts for mental health. (n.d.-a). Port St Lucie Hospital Inc. https://www.portstluciehospitalinc.com/10-journaling-prompts-for-mental-health/&ved=2ahUKEwj-qKX20b3-AhWC-6QKHVvrCwsQFnoECAwQAQ&usg=AOvVaw2s Rbvh963pZBEGjtQHNEk-

Journaling prompts for mental health. (n.d.-b). Mindful Health Solutions. https://mindfulhealthsolutions.com/20-journaling-prompts-for-mental-health/&ved=2ahUKEwj-qKX20b3-AhWC-6QKHVvrCwsQFnoECAcQBQ&usg=AOvVaw3vhK8w 8tXWpBKxdlBRZXJV

Kristenson, S. (2022, April 6). *60 encouraging affirmations to move on after a breakup.* Happier Human. https://www.happierhum an.com/affirmations-breakup/&ved=2ahUKEwiRk_LC0b3-AhXLOuwKHccWA4MQFnoECA4QAQ&usg=AOvVaw311Nf rkDAM3lgGGc2omf3F

Kristenson, S. (2023, February 27). *9 steps to be happy after a painful breakup.* Happier Human. https://www.happierhuman.com/happy-breakup-wa1/&ved=2ahUKEwi0j4mkpL3-AhXEtKQK HctQAqs4ChAWegQIBRAB&usg=AOvVaw2sGiD6sWYiVw6 Kjpy0DicT

Lamonthe, C., & Raypole, C. (2023, July 13). *Is your relationship toxic? What to look for.* Healthline. https://www.healthline.com/ health/toxic-relationship&ved=2ahUKEwjssMWRor3- AhVpMewKHecZCJcQFnoECCMQAQ&usg=AOvVaw1DbVV V9SSSNO6uEd-vakrK

Lawler, M. (2023, February 8). *How to get over a breakup: 7 things therapists want you to know.* Everyday Health. https://www.eve rydayhealth.com/emotional-health/how-move-on-10-steps- closure-after-you-break-up/&ved=2ahUKEwighKbKpL3- AhUNJOwKHSidBsgQFnoECCsQAQ&usg=AOvVaw1rJuUiudj nnCDhb3tIAJCL

Livingstone, B. (2011, September 23). *Is it love or addiction?* MentalHelp. https://www.mentalhelp.net/blogs/is-it-love-or-addiction/

Lovine, A. (2021, August 16). *How to start dating again after a break.* Mashable. https://mashable.com/article/how-to-date-again- after-break&ved=2ahUKEwjh0ueEoL3-AhUCzqQKHf0lBxcQ FnoECCQQAQ&usg=AOvVaw1T4M8IN3sQYQwuTUO1dJku

Marturana Winderl, A. (n.d.). *6 smart ways to boost your self-esteem.* Wonder Mind. https://www.wondermind.com/article/boost- your-self-esteem/&ved=2ahUKEwjqxbvd073-AhXM1qQKH ZRdAIQ4ChAWegQIDxAB&usg=AOvVaw2-LmxGdPfby BKOEz5bo_TO

MasterClass. (2022, August 3). *How to build a habit: 7 tips for building good habits.* MasterClass. https://www.masterclass.com/ articles/how-to-build-a-habit&ved=2ahUKEwi_5Jf20L3- AhUCPOwKHdj3AOEQFnoECC0QAQ&usg=AOvVaw2O47ZI r-NqNz7qdP_Xz1yw

Mendez, J. (2020, February 7). *Breakups are painful, but they can lead to important self-discovery. here are 4 questions to ask yourself after a heartbreak.* Business Insider. https://www.businessinsider .com/questions-to-ask-yourself-after-breakup-self-discovery%3 Famp&ved=2ahUKEwiy27rX1L3-AhUF7KQKHa8NDJMQFno ECCoQAQ&usg=AOvVaw3765ivW3xCzru64w-nAHIW

Millacci, T. S. (2023, April 6). *Healthy coping: 24 mechanisms & skills for positive coping.* Positive Psychology. https://positivepsy chology.com/coping/&ved=2ahUKEwjHkrWBzb3- AhVVs6QKHTKlDhAQFnoECFkQAQ&usg=AOvVaw00wokL D34mZJGXiD9xC5dq

Miller, R. (2018, August 30). *Reclaiming your independence post-breakup.* A Healthier Michigan. https://www.ahealthiermichigan.org/ 2018/08/30/reclaiming-your-independence-post-breakup/ &ved=2ahUKEwjgteiH1L3-AhUpuaQKHQkvCokQFnoECC0 QAQ&usg=AOvVaw2cUM43phk6bCXHNQFH0JE7

Mindful Staff. (2023, January 6). *Mindfulness meditation: How to do it.* Mindful. https://www.mindful.org/mindfulness-how-to-do- it/&ved=2ahUKEwipvbeK0L3-AhVPPOwKHZ9mD_AQFno ECD8QAQ&usg=AOvVaw1dtldb5WGy8xYrLpHirhSj

Mindfulness exercises. (n.d.). Mayo Clinic. https://www.mayoclinic.org/ healthy-lifestyle/consumer-health/in-depth/mindfulness-exercises/ art-20046356&ved=2ahUKEwipvbeK0L3-AhVPPOwKHZ9mD_ AQFnoECA0QBQ&usg=AOvVaw0g_f3cOWRVDB-K4Le1gRm3

Mindfulness meditation techniques. (n.d.). Mindfulness Meditation Institute. https://mindfulnessmeditationinstitute.org/the-mind fulness-meditation-practice/mindfulness-meditation-techniq

ues/&ved=2ahUKEwipvbeK0L3-AhVPPOwKHZ9mD_AQFno
ECCAQAQ&usg=AOvVaw2jPuDMM9RBHJlfW3IpZfzI

MindTools Content Team. (n.d.). *How to build self-confidence.* MindTools.
https://www.mindtools.com/ap5omwt/how-to-build-self-confide
nce&ved=2ahUKEwiFvorv073-AhWE-KQKHdDwCaIQFnoECG
wQAQ&usg=AOvVaw3gMsnlVUqOPmYRctyWKnaw

Minor, J. (n.d.). *Boundaries worksheets.* Pinterest. https://www.pintere
st.com/pin/boundaries-worksheets7--3096293486137327/&ved
=2ahUKEwje2uDqpL3-AhWL2KQKHekNA0IQFnoECE8QAQ
&usg=AOvVaw3QgTpgZ56r_3SHq-f4gWLS

Moeller, S. (2017). *Forgiveness after a breakup.* Grief Recovery Method.
https://www.griefrecoverymethod.com/blog/2017/07/forgivenes
s-after-breakup&ved=2ahUKEwid1tCNz73-AhUPOewKH
chhC98QFnoECA4QAQ&usg=AOvVaw1A5-5hwSTofFgT
U3Ey0chH

Moore, M. (n.d.). *4 examples of boundaries with an ex.* Psych Central.
https://psychcentral.com/relationships/set-boundaries-with-
your-ex&ved=2ahUKEwiT3KL1o73-AhVtMewKHXUjCmMQF
noECCUQAQ&usg=AOvVaw38kRiQYbR56B97jmZGm_a8

Mudge, L. (2023, February 2). *Why does heartbreak hurt so much?
Science has the answer.* Livescience. https://www.livescienc
e.com/why-does-heartbreak-hurt-so-much#:~:text=These%20n
egative%20emotions%20are%20influenced

Mulligan, M. (2021, December 21). *The 7 most toxic relationship
patterns—and how to break them for good.* Red Book.
https://www.redbookmag.com/love-sex/relationships/

g3064/the-7-unhealthy-relationship-patterns/&ved=2ahUK
EwjssMWRor3-AhVpMewKHecZCJcQFnoECCAQAQ&usg=A
OvVaw1US1ZbSnmwjI-ftz_o-fc8

Naftulin, J. (2021, May 26). *5 signs you're ready to start dating again
after a breakup, according to relationship therapists.* Insider.
https://www.insider.com/signs-you-are-ready-to-date-again-
after-breakup-advice-2021-5%3Famp&ved=2ahUKEwjh0
ueEoL3-AhUCzqQKHf0lBxcQFnoECCUQAQ&usg=A
OvVaw3Ca4WIGnplBa35T4hu853I

Nash, J. (2023). *Building healthy relationships with 40 helpful worksheets.*
Positive Psychology. https://positivepsychology.com/healthy-
relationships-worksheets/&ved=2ahUKEwiEh_nDor3-
AhUKrKQKHUj9BB4QFnoECCMQAQ&usg=AOvVaw3Ii0_DSq
TENP8LkXYw-gcU

Neff, K., & Germer, C. (2019, January 29). *The transformative effects of
mindful self-compassion.* Mindful. https://www.mindful.org/the-
transformative-effects-of-mindful-self-compassion/

NHS. (n.d.). *Raising low self-esteem.* NHS. https://www.nhs.uk/mental-
health/self-help/tips-and-support/raise-low-self-esteem/&ved=
2ahUKEwix9aCz073-AhWkOOwKHb1VAtkQFnoECCEQAQ
&usg=AOvVaw0ShApiGlSJE4FuK-taby4V

Njuguna, A. B. (2023, January 31). *The nature of forgiveness and the
benefits of forgiving your ex.* Paired Life. https://pairedlife.com/
breakups/advantages-of-forgiveness-after-a-break-
up&ved=2ahUKEwid1tCNz73-AhUPOewKHchhC98QF
noECA0QAQ&usg=AOvVaw2DcotBRj7sCaKuq-LLrm2S

Novak, A. (2017, July 27). *How to use mindfulness to get through a breakup.* The Thirty. https://thethirty.whowhatwear.com/mindfulness-breakup&ved=2ahUKEwjp0YOrz73-AhUNH-wKHcf7B444ChAWegQIAxAB&usg=AOvVaw3J-mv8odfBD60l3sPHDnNc

Nunez, A. (n.d.). *Rebuilding yourself after heartbreak.* Revoloon. https://revoloon.com/angnunez/rebuilding-after-heartbreak&ved=2ahUKEwjgteiH1L3-AhUpuaQKHQkvCokQFnoECC4QAQ&usg=AOvVaw0i9B5L7tqFYShEUAlLbJBP

Pan, M. (2021, March 19). *The 4 most common toxic dating patterns and how to identify them.* Medium. https://medium.com/hello-love/the-4-most-common-toxic-dating-patterns-and-how-to-identify-them-2bfd80fb5cd5&ved=2ahUKEwjssMWRor3-AhVpMewKHecZCJcQFnoECCUQAQ&usg=AOvVaw1JWCstOMCSei51O4Odzm48

Paula. (2023). *10 strategies for effective communication.* I'm Busy Being Awesome. https://imbusybeingawesome.com/10-strategies-for-effective-communication/&ved=2ahUKEwiQjcT3ob3-AhXgxwIHHfMZAM8QFnoECAkQBQ&usg=AOvVaw0DonIXLeQbZg_Ow4m6hYY5

Perry, E. (2022, March 30). *How to improve self-esteem: 8 tips to give you a boost.* Better Up. https://www.betterup.com/blog/how-to-improve-self-esteem%3Fhs_amp%3Dtrue&ved=2ahUKEwjryPjN073-AhUQuaQKHYrcBE0QFnoECE4QAQ&usg=AovVaw2B4-ou45LLdVypeDVE5zkP

Personal growth: Embracing the challenges of self-discovery for a more fulfilling life. (n.d.). Pebble Galaxy. https://pebblegalaxy.blog/

2023/04/18/personal-growth-embracing-the-challenges-of-self-discovery-for-a-more-fulfilling-life/%23:~:text%3DConclusion-

Phoenix, O. (2020, April 7). *Meditation helps to overcome a broken heart.* The Way of Meditation. https://www.thewayofmedit ation.com.au/meditation-helps-to-overcome-a-broken-heart &ved=2ahUKEwjp0YOrz73-AhUNH-wKHcf7B444ChAWe gQIBRAB&usg=AOvVaw124n73xucpwFpZ2jdTeEHD

Positive affirmations to help heal your broken heart. (n.d.). The Positive Mom. https://www.thepositivemom.com/positive-affirmations-to-help-heal-your-broken-heart&ved=2ahUKEwiRk_LC0b3-AhXLOuwKHccWA4MQFnoECAkQAQ&usg=AOvVaw1lT14 2RrwGarnbmjdl9X-h

Printable self-care worksheets for your planner. (n.d.). Project Energise. https://projectenergise.com/printable-self-care-worksheets-2/&ved=2ahUKEwiwvZOz0r3-AhUbxgIHHRplAmY QFnoECB4QAQ&usg=AOvVaw0Qgi3zBnrECB5_zzYraJ1j

Quinn, D. (2022, December 29). *What does withdrawal feel like?: Everything you need to know & when to go to detox.* Sandstone Care. https://www.sandstonecare.com/blog/what-does-withdrawal-feel-like-2/

Rachel. (2021, September 26). *9 self-reflecting questions to ask yourself after a breakup.* Doctor for Love. https://www.doctorforlove .com/9-self-reflecting-questions-to-ask-yourself-after-a-breakup/&ved=2ahUKEwiy27rX1L3-AhUF7KQKHa8NDJMQ FnoECCgQAQ&usg=AOvVaw2BDujMQIXtZcRs50ok3t5Q

Raypole, C. (2021, August 26). *The beginner's guide to trauma responses.* Healthline. https://www.healthline.com/health/ mental-health/fight-flight-freeze-fawn&ved=2ahUKEwj5wu7k zL3-AhWStKQKHQIgChUQFnoECBgQAQ&usg=AOvVaw2SF 5zmrsq32wFqaxv5QyNS

Reid, S. (n.d.). *Setting healthy boundaries in relationships.* Help Guide. https://www.helpguide.org/articles/relationships-communication/setting-healthy-boundaries-in-relationships.htm&ved=2ahUKEwiUk_Ckob3-AhUhMuwKHWqvAgMQFnoECD4QAQ&usg=AOvVaw3w9w Ici0w5Wp8-ZZbmYKX2

Relationships and communication. (2023). Better Health. https://www.betterhealth.vic.gov.au/health/healthyliving/relatio nships-and-communication&ved=2ahUKEwiQjcT3ob3-AhXgxwIHHfMZAM8QFnoECA0QBQ&usg=AOvVaw3ULam E3_pVf689bNkepmuS

Richardsson, J. (n.d.). *Healthy coping strategies for mental health.* 29K. https://29k.org/healthy-coping-strategies-for-mental-health&ved=2ahUKEwiG6IDb0L3-AhXHNOwKHVKbCRMQFnoECBYQAQ&usg=AOvVaw3q21 8cDZCAyIjv5Oe62bkb

RTE. (2022). *A counselling psychologists guide to heartbreak.* RTE. https://www.rte.ie/lifestyle/living/2022/0902/1319492-a-counselling-psychologists-guide-to-heartbreak/&ved=2ahUKEwiB5Z6lzr3-AhXosaQKHU3WDQM4FBAWegQIBBAB&usg=AOvVaw0Y5 38o00SEmQhVwRyWgM_p

Saad, S. K. (2021, May 25). *How to heal your broken heart when it literally feels impossible.* Cosmopolitan. https://www.cosmo politan.com/sex-love/a36532827/how-to-heal-a-broken-heart/&ved=2ahUKEwifrIjvzb3-AhWHtqQKHd90BmwQ FnoECCsQAQ&usg=AOvVaw2uX9508lKuwOzeimqWP-RD

Schaeffer, A. (2016, March 16). *How does heartbreak affect your overall health?* Healthline. https://www.healthline.com/health/what-does-heartbreak-do-to-your-health%23:~:text%3D%25E2%2 580%259CDepression%252C%2520anxiety%252C%2520and%2 520withdrawal

Schaffner, A. K. (2020, May 20). *How to practice self-care: 10+ worksheets and 12 ideas.* Positive Psychology. https://positivepsychology.com/self-care-worksheets/&ved=2ahUKEwiwvZOz0r3-AhUbxgIHHRplAm YQFnoECCEQAQ&usg=AOvVaw0kdKfDrZBeB7u2wPIEN-4a

Schewietz, S. (2022, September 22). *How long should you wait to date after a breakup? Expert advice on the best time to move on.* WikiHow. https://www.wikihow.com/How-Long-Should-You-Wait-to-Date-After-a-Breakup%23:~:text%3DWait%2520at %2520least%25203%2520months%2520before%2520you%2520 start%2520dating%2520again.%26text%3DIf%2520you%27ve% 2520broken%2520up

Scott, E. (2022, January 12). *How to improve your relationships with effective communication skills.* Very Well Mind. https://www.verywellmind.com/managing-conflict-in-relation ships-communication-tips-3144967&ved=2ahUKEwiQjcT 3ob3-AhXgxwIHHfMZAM8QFnoECCkQAQ&usg=AOvVaw3- -EyuEiEOyZWH9wn_d3AI

Scott, E. (2023, February 13). *5 self-care practices for every area of your life.* Very Well Mind. https://www.verywellmind.com/self-care-strategies-overall-stress-reduction-3144729&ved=2ahUKEwi qxNiT0b3-AhWfxQIHHY63AfsQFnoECCkQAQ&usg=A OvVaw0LnVx8TOEQjJdQK_kV6uAM

Seattle Christian Counseling. (2020, August 19). *7 keys to effective communication skills in relationships.* Seattle Christian Counseling. https://seattlechristiancounseling.com/articles/7-keys-to-effective-communication-skills-in-relationships&ved=2 ahUKEwiQjcT3ob3-AhXgxwIHHfMZAM8QFnoECCYQAQ& usg=AOvVaw3a9N4Dq0plD_k6vcCEpgnZ

Sekendur, B. (n.d.). *Healing, forgiving, and loving after a painful break up.* Tiny Buddha. https://tinybuddha.com/blog/healing-forgiving-and-loving-after-a-near-death-break-up/&ved=2ahUKEwid1tC Nz73-AhUPOewKHchhC98QFnoECAwQAQ&usg=AOvVaw3 W0gss4gFJu68YRfoXVMV8

Self-Esteem worksheets: Fill your emotional cup with self-care. (n.d.). Teachers Pay Teachers. https://www.teacherspayteachers.com/ Product/Self-Esteem-Worksheets-Fill-Your-Emotional-Cup-with-Self-Care-3565903&ved=2ahUKEwjnxei_0r3-AhUQ3qQKHWUrCgQ4ChAWegQICRAB&usg=AOvVaw092 CzHbI1oq22kHN8HX429

Setting better boundaries. (n.d.). Embodied Psychology. http://www.embodiedpsychology.ca/setting-better-boundaries-downloadable-handouts.html&ved=2ahUKEwj47N31pL3-AhUaPOwKHUSmCCc4ChAWegQIBBAB&usg=AOvVaw2Vy SdCl_a5L623nl76gc5P

Setting boundaries: Info and practice. (n.d.). Therapist Aid.
https://www.therapistaid.com/therapy-worksheet/setting-
boundaries&ved=2ahUKEwje2uDqpL3-AhWL2KQKHekNA0I
QFnoECA0QAQ&usg=AOvVaw3RRUIBRM3XttORSJyfKcR4

Smith, S. (n.d.). *How to get closure after a breakup: 10 step guide.*
Marriage. https://www.marriage.com/advice/relationship/how-
to-get-closure-after-a-breakup/&ved=2ahUKEwighKbKpL3-
AhUNJOwKHSidBsgQFnoECC4QAQ&usg=AOvVaw1gPmX
WgDM9zrJBMdJJZdaU

St. Claire, C. (2014). *The 7-step guide that will turn your breakup into
the best thing that's ever happened to you.* Thought Catalog.
https://thoughtcatalog.com/claudia-st-clair/2014/03/the-7-step-
guide-that-will-turn-your-breakup-into-the-best-thing-thats-
ever-happened-to-you/&ved=2ahUKEwiWuuvXo73-
AhVN_KQKHQ9rDgEQFnoECAkQAQ&usg=AOvVaw2IhFzc
Kap_Ylhg3yic800V

Sutton, J. (2018, May 18). *5 benefits of journaling for mental health.*
Positive Psychology. https://positivepsychology.com/benefits-
of-journaling/&ved=2ahUKEwjTnrjb0b3-AhULPuwKHXb2BlI
QFnoECBgQAQ&usg=AOvVaw3cPJW58VznZ4Ia5GZ4VBya

Tartakovsky, M. (2022, February 22). *6 journaling benefits and how to
start right now.* Healthline. https://www.healthline.com/
health/benefits-of-journaling&ved=2ahUKEwjTnrjb0b3-
AhULPuwKHXb2BlIQFnoECB0QAQ&usg=AOvVaw0rjgwjHV
Ml342IJOB8P-mW

Therapy worksheets. (2023). Therapist Aid. https://www.therapistaid
.com/therapy-worksheets/relationships/none&ved=2ahUKE

wiEh_nDor3-AhUKrKQKHUj9BB4QFnoECA0QAQ&
usg=AOvVaw2N8jFY-U0u_naGHViITlgI

Therapy worksheets to streamline your mental health practice. (n.d.).
Therapy by Pro. https://therapybypro.com/product-category/
template/&ved=2ahUKEwjizv70z73-AhVMsaQKHWxLCyk4K
BAWegQICxAB&usg=AOvVaw15GmhLlowDetX4TBUbqRk9

This is Calmer. (n.d.). *The power of positive thinking and affirmations.*
This Is Calmer. https://www.thisiscalmer.com/blog/the-power-
of-positive-thinking-and-affirmations&ved=2ahUKEwjF99-
n0b3-AhUPJewKHQcyD2UQFnoECCUQAQ&usg=AOv
Vaw0Y5f3I42rY8LXX4IuEudBu

Top 3 easy self-discovery exercises you need to try. (n.d.). Cresentella.
https://cresentella.com/self-discovery-exercises/&ved=2ahUK
EwjA1tjI1b3-AhWTtqQKHTw4AN04ChAWegQIBhAB&
usg=AOvVaw0gE5kikpRvTX9_YJEUSmWb

Top tips on building and maintaining healthy relationships. (n.d.).
Mental Health. https://www.mentalhealth.org.uk/our-work/
public-engagement/healthy-relationships/top-tips-building-
and-maintaining-healthy-relationships&ved=2ahUKEwjghceP
ob3-AhXPFOwKHXtmDS0QFnoECFYQAQ&usg=AOvVaw0y-
isH73Qn0cBqRCilsUcm

Trauma: It's more than just "fight or flight." (n.d.). PTSD UK.
https://www.ptsduk.org/its-so-much-more-than-just-fight-or-
flight/&ved=2ahUKEwj5wu7kzL3-AhWStKQKHQIgChUQF
noECCoQAQ&usg=AOvVaw0tisdkN4C4R1kG4qU_NX_t

Tull, M. (2020, April 27). *The link between PTSD and fight or flight
response.* Very Well Mind. https://www.verywellmind.com/

ptsd-and-the-fight-or-flight-response-2797642&ved=2ahUKE
wj5wu7kzL3-AhWStKQKHQIgChUQFnoECCwQAQ&usg=
AOvVaw1SLAsDYOLQov7v5AgeOSL2

Vincenty, S. (2022, January 17). *How to get over a breakup, according to experts.* Oprah Daily. https://www.oprahdaily.com/life/ relationships-love/a28748535/what-to-do-after-breakup/&ved =2ahUKEwjfgPWto73-AhVH66QKHXieByIQFnoECDUQ AQ&usg=AOvVaw2P8QbMuCLe_OEKvmanLYA6

Wahome, C. (2021, August 26). *How to love again after a breakup.* WebMd. https://www.webmd.com/sex-relationships/features/ how-to-love-again-after-a-breakup&ved=2ahUKEwil6bOioL3- AhUIxQIHHSXJDWIQFnoECCgQAQ&usg=AOvVaw2Nx6vlY T2II3E14VBMjvAt

Walter, M. (n.d.). *If you want closure after a breakup: 6 things you need to know.* Tiny Buddha. https://tinybuddha.com/blog/want- closure-breakup-6-things-need-know/&ved=2ahUKEwigh KbKpL3-AhUNJOwKHSidBsgQFnoECCgQAQ&usg=AOv Vaw0PEotNz0FL9l5uHkoLX1q8

What does a healthy relationship look like? (n.d.). New York State. https://www.ny.gov/teen-dating-violence-awareness-and- prevention/what-does-healthy-relationship-look%23:~:text %3DHealthy%2520relationships%2520involve%2520honesty%2 52C%2520trust

What is psychotherapy? (n.d.). Psychotherapy. https://www.psychother apy.org.uk/seeking-therapy/what-is-psychotherapy/&ved= 2ahUKEwib9Kjizr3-AhVMUcAKHTZQB1IQFnoECCoQAQ& usg=AOvVaw1cbf-1TeeGOjGAAVyIOO_-

Where do broken hearts go? (n.d.). Benenden. https://www.benenden
.co.uk/be-healthy/mind/where-do-broken-hearts-
go/&ved=2ahUKEwizvtLXzb3-AhXG2KQKHcg3BLAQ
FnoECCgQAQ&usg=AOvVaw1o9RGsyq0fpleFuNFHHOpp

White, L. (n.d.). *6 essential breakup boundaries.* Belief Net.
https://www.beliefnet.com/love-family/relationships/dating/6-
essential-breakup-boundaries.aspx&ved=2ahUKEwiT3KL1o73-
AhVtMewKHXUjCmMQFnoECCEQAQ&usg=AOvVaw0BiN
w3GC_W7Nl1Sx737e2U

Wiebe, J. (2019, April 10). *5 ways to strengthen your support system.*
Talk Space. https://www.talkspace.com/blog/how-to-
strengthen-your-support-system/&ved=2ahUKEwjEoLWU0r3-
AhUlMewKHX9mBv0QFnoECAgQBQ&usg=AOvVaw0BFVx3
04uTC43J83jVb4O2

Wilson, G. (2018, March 23). *Why a breakup feels like a drug withdrawal.*
SBS News. https://www.sbs.com.au/news/insight/article/why-a-
breakup-feels-like-a-drug-withdrawal/srqjenmpv

Winch, G. (2018, January 7). *3 surprising ways heartbreak impacts your
brain.* Psychology Today. https://www.psychologytoday.com/intl/bl
og/the-squeaky-wheel/201801/3-surprising-ways-heartbreak-impac
ts-your-brain%3Famp&ved=2ahUKEwjh4PO0zL3-AhWIjaQKHT
mOAvQQFnoECCkQAQ&usg=AovVaw0IrnibL9tnEpCl1oGta9Qf

Wong, K. (2023, January 28). *30 affirmations for healing after a
breakup.* Millennial Grind. https://millennial-grind.com/30-
affirmations-for-healing-after-breakup/&ved=2ahUKEwiRk
_LC0b3-AhXLOuwKHccWA4MQFnoECCsQAQ&usg=AovV
aw3NS7ZFLLsOTew2UCM_b9Jt

Worksheets to help those coping with grief. (2020, September 4). Guide
  Peacefully. https://guide.peacefully.com/resources/worksheets-
  to-help-those-coping-with-grief&ved=2ahUKEwjizv70z73-
  AhVMsaQKHWxLCyk4KBAWegQIBhAB&usg=AOvVaw0Cgv
  6qaoCqLiJgOEZNq1rE

Young, K. (n.d.). Recovering from a breakup: Proven ways to heal
  (from science). Hey Sigmund. https://www.heysigmund.com/
  recovering-from-a-breakup/&ved=2ahUKEwifrIjvzb3-AhWHtq
  QKHd90BmwQFnoECCcQAQ&usg=AOvVaw3l946a49fugAZ
  VRtg8c2xU

Printed in Great Britain
by Amazon